PENGUIN POETS

D67

# CONTEMPORARY AMERICAN POETRY

## SELECTED BY DONALD HALL

# CONTEMPORARY
# AMERICAN POETRY

SELECTED AND INTRODUCED BY
DONALD HALL

PENGUIN BOOKS

BALTIMORE · MARYLAND

Penguin Books Inc
7110 Ambassador Road
Baltimore, Maryland 21207

First published 1962
Reprinted 1964, 1965, 1966, 1967, 1968, 1969, 1970

Cover Design by Stephen Russ

Printed in the United States of America

# CONTENTS

WILLIAM STAFFORD (b. 1914) comes from Kansas and
was educated at the Universities of Kansas, Wisconsin,
and Iowa. He has taught in California and Indiana, and is
now at Lewis and Clark College in Oregon. *West of Your
City* appeared in 1960, and *Travelling through the Dark* in
1962.

ROBERT LOWELL (b. 1917) is a member of the Bostonian
family which included a President of Harvard and the poets
Amy and James Russell. He attended Harvard and Kenyon,
and studied with John Crowe Ransom. After returning to
live in Boston for several years, Lowell has recently moved
to New York City. His first book, *Land of Unlikeness*, was
issued in a small edition by the Cummington Press in 1944.
The best of these poems were revised to appear in *Lord
Weary's Castle* 1946, Lowell's first full-scale book, which
won the Pulitzer Prize for Poetry in 1947. *The Mills of the
Kavanaghs* followed in 1951, and *Life Studies* (which won
the National Book Award) in 1959. A book of translations,
*Imitations*, appeared in 1961.

ROBERT DUNCAN (b. 1919) comes from Oakland, California, and has continued to live nearby. He has edited the *Experimental Review* and *Phoenix*, and taught at Black Mountain College. Among his books are *Letters* (1958), *Selected Poems* (1959), and *The Opening of the Field* (1960).

REED WHITTEMORE (b. 1919) was born in New Haven, Connecticut, and attended Yale University. He now teaches at Carleton College in Northfield, Minnesota. He edited *Furioso* (1939–53) and edits *The Carleton Miscellany*, both literary quarterlies of considerable humour. His books of poems are *Heroes and Heroines* (1946), *An American Takes a Walk* (1956), *The Self-made Man and Other Poems* (1959), and *The Boy From Iowa* (1962).

HOWARD NEMEROV (b. 1920) joined the Royal Canadian Air Force after graduating from Harvard, and flew in England during the war. He has published considerable literary criticism, three novels, and a book of short stories as well as his books of poems: *The Image and The Law* (1947), *Guide to the Ruins* (1950), *The Salt Garden* (1955), *Mirrors and Windows* (1958), and *New and Selected Poems* (1960). He teaches at Bennington College in Vermont.

RICHARD WILBUR (b. 1921) was educated at Amherst
College and fought in the Signal Corps in Anzio and
France. Then he attended Harvard, where he took an M.A.
in 1947, and was a Junior Fellow in the Society of Fellows
1947–50. He has taught at Harvard, Wellesley, and Wes-
leyan University, and he has been a Guggenheim Fellow
and received a Prix de Rome. His books of poems are *The
Beautiful Changes* (1947), *Ceremony* (1950), *Things of this
World* (1956), *Poems 1943–1956* (England) (1957), and
*Advice to a Prophet* (1961). In 1957 he received the
Pulitzer Prize and the National Book Award for *Things of
this World*.

ANTHONY HECHT (b. 1922) is a native of New York
City and attended Kenyon College, where he studied with
John Crowe Ransom. He fought with the American
infantry in Europe in the Second World War, and more recently has taught at Smith College. He has been a Guggenheim Fellow and a Hudson Review Fellow. *A Summoning
of Stones* appeared in 1954.

JAMES DICKEY (b. 1923) was born in Georgia and has
lived most of his life in the South. He flew in the Pacific

during the war and afterwards taught and worked for an advertising agency. He has been a Guggenheim Fellow and a Sewanee Review Fellow. His books are *Unto the Stone and Other Poems* (1960) and *Drowning with Others* (1962).

DENISE LEVERTOV (b. 1923) comes from Ilford in Essex, England, and served as a nurse during the Second World War, when her poems were first published by Wrey Gardiner in London. She married an American and has lived in the United States since 1948. She published her first book, *The Double Image*, in England in 1946. Her American books are *Here and Now* (1957), *Overland to the Islands* (1958), *With Eyes at the Back of our Heads* (1960), and *The Jacob's Ladder* (1961).

JOHN LOGAN (b. 1923) is the editor of *Chicago Choice* and teaches at Notre Dame University. His books of poems are *Cycle for Mother Cabrini* (1955), and *Ghosts of the Heart* (1960).

LOUIS SIMPSON (b. 1923), born in Jamaica in the West Indies, came to the United States in 1940, and attended Columbia University. He spent three years in the United States Army, mostly in glider infantry, and received his citizenship at Berchtesgaden. He has been a publisher and is now teaching at the University of California, Berkeley. He has had a Hudson Review Fellowship and a Prix de Rome. His published works include a novel, a critical

# CONTENTS

study of James Hogg, and three books of poems: *The Arrivistes* (1950), *Good News of Death and Other Poems* (1955), and *A Dream of Governors* (1959).

EDGAR BOWERS (b. 1924) was born in Georgia, and attended the University of North Carolina and Stanford, where he studied with Yvor Winters. He fought through Germany in the Second World War. He has been a Sewanee Review Fellow and a Guggenheim Fellow. He now teaches at the University of California, Santa Barbara. His book of poems is *The Form of Loss* (1956).

DONALD JUSTICE (b. 1925) was born in Miami, Florida, where he attended the University of Miami. He has studied at Stanford University and the University of North Carolina, and is now teaching at the State University of Iowa. He has had a Rockefeller Fellowship in poetry. He published *The Summer Anniversaries*, which was the Lamont Poetry Selection, in 1959.

# CONTENTS

ROBERT BLY (b. 1926) was born on the Western plains of Minnesota, and attended St Olaf's College and Harvard University. He is editor of the literary magazine, *The Sixties*, and has spent a year in Norway on a Fulbright award. He has translated poems from various languages, and translates Scandinavian prose for the New American Library and other publishers.

ROBERT CREELEY (b. 1926), was raised in Massachusetts, attended Harvard, and served in India and Burma with the American Field Service during the war. In recent years he has lived in France, Spain, and Guatemala, where he has edited and taught school. He has taught at Black Mountain College and done graduate work at the University of New Mexico. His books include *The Whip* (1957), *A Form of Women* (1959), and *For Love* (*Poems 1950–1960*) (1962).

JAMES MERRILL (b. 1926) is a graduate of Amherst College, and lives in Stonington, Connecticut. He has published one novel, *The Seraglio*, and two books of poems in the United States: *First Poems* (1951), and *The Country of a Thousand Years of Peace* (1959). *Poems 1948–1961* appeared in England in 1962.

W. D. SNODGRASS (b. 1926) grew up in Beaver Falls, Pennsylvania, where he majored in music at Geneva College. After service in the Navy he attended the State University of Iowa, and taught at Cornell and Rochester. He is now teaching at Wayne State University in Detroit. He won an award for his poetry from the Ingram Merrill Foundation and has had a Hudson Review Fellowship. His book of poems, *Heart's Needle* (1959), received the Pulitzer Prize for Poetry in 1960.

JOHN ASHBERY (b. 1927), a native of Sodus, New York, was educated at Deerfield and Harvard. He has worked for *Art News* and is now on the staff of the Paris Edition of the New York Herald Tribune. Three of his plays have been produced by art theatres, and he has published two principal collections of his poems, *Some Trees* (Yale Series of Younger Poets, 1956) and *The Tennis Court Oath* (1962).

CONTENTS

GALWAY KINNELL (b. 1927) was born in Rhode Island
and attended Princeton University. He has lived in France
where he taught at Grenoble, and in Iran. He has translated
Yves Bonnefoy and other French poets. He published
*What a Kingdom It Was*, his first book of poems, in 1960.

W. S. MERWIN (b. 1927) was born in New York City,
raised in Pennsylvania, and educated at Princeton University. He has spent most of the past decade in Spain,
England, and France. He has written several plays for
radio and the stage, and has published numerous translations from the Spanish and the French. His four books of
poems are *A Mask for Janus* (Yale Series of Younger
Poets, 1952), *The Dancing Bears* (1954), *Green with
Beasts* (1956), and *The Drunk in the Furnace* (1960).

JAMES WRIGHT (b. 1927) is a native of Ohio, and studied
at Kenyon College and the University of Washington. He
has been a Kenyon Review Fellow and has lived in
Austria on a Fulbright award. He teaches at the University
of Minnesota. His books of poems are *The Green Wall*
(Yale Series of Younger Poets, 1957), and *Saint Judas*
(1959).

X. J. KENNEDY (b. 1929) is a native of New Jersey and took his B.A. at Seton Hall University. He spent four years in the U.S. Navy and a year in Paris before going to the University of Michigan for graduate study. He won a major Hopwood Award there in 1959. His first book of poems, *Nude Descending a Staircase*, was the Lamont Poetry Selection for 1961.

ADRIENNE RICH (b. 1929), a native of Baltimore, published her first book of poems when she was a senior at Radcliffe College. She is married to a Professor at Harvard and lives in Cambridge. She has been a Guggenheim Fellow and has held an Amy Lowell Travelling Scholarship. Her two books are *A Change of World* (Yale Series of Younger Poets, 1951) and *The Diamond Cutters* (1955).

GARY SNYDER (b. 1930), who was born in San Francisco and raised in Washington, attended Reed College, Indiana University and the University of California, Berkeley. He is now living in Japan. His books are *Riprap* (1959) and *Myths and Texts* (1960).

# CONTENTS

ROBERT MEZEY (b. 1935) is a native of Philadelphia, who
attended Kenyon College and the State University of
Iowa. He is now living in Tennessee. *The Lovemaker*
appeared in 1961, and was the Lamont Poetry Selection
for 1960.

# ACKNOWLEDGEMENTS

FOR permission to publish or reproduce the poems in this anthology, acknowledgement is made to the following:

For John Ashbery to the author, Yale University Press for 'The Picture of Little J.A. in a Prospect of Flowers' and 'Some Trees', from *Some Trees*, and Wesleyan University Press for 'Thoughts of a Young Girl' and 'Our Youth', Copyright John Ashbery 1962, from *The Tennis Court Oath* by John Ashbery; for Robert Bly to the author; for Edgar Bowers to the author and Alan Swallow, the publisher, for 'The Prince' and 'The Mountain Cemetery', from *The Form of Loss* by Edgar Bowers, Copyright Edgar Bowers 1954; for Robert Creeley to the author and Charles Scribner's Sons for poems from *For Love* by Robert Creeley, Copyright Robert Creeley; for James Dickey to the author and Charles Scribner's Sons for 'The Performance', Copyright 1959 The Modern Poetry Society, from POETS OF TODAY VII, *Into the Stone and Other Poems* by James Dickey; for Robert Duncan to the author and Grove Press, Inc. for 'A Poem Beginning with a Line by Pindar', from *The Opening of the Field* by Robert Duncan, Copyright Robert Duncan 1960; for Anthony Hecht to the author and The Macmillan Company for 'Samuel Sewall' and 'Alceste in the Wilderness', from *A Summoning of Stones* by Anthony Hecht; for Donald Justice to the author and Wesleyan University Press for poems from *The Summer Anniversaries* by Donald Justice, Copyright Donald Justice, 1954, 1956, 1959; for X. J. Kennedy to the author and Doubleday and Co. Inc. for poems from *Nude Descending a Staircase* by X. J. Kennedy, Copyright X. J. Kennedy 1960, 1961; for Galway Kinnell to Houghton Mifflin Co. and the author; for Denise Levertov to the author; for John Logan to the author and the University of Chicago Press for 'The Picnic' and 'A Trip to Four or Five Towns', from *Ghosts of the Heart* by John Logan; for Robert Lowell to Faber and Faber Ltd, the author, Farrar, Straus and Cudahy Inc. for poems from *Life Studies* by Robert Lowell, Copyright Robert Lowell 1956, 1959, and Harcourt, Brace and World, Inc. for poems from *Lord Weary's Castle* by Robert Lowell, Copyright Robert Lowell 1956, 1959; for James Merrill to the *New Yorker* and the author; for W. S. Merwin to Rupert Hart-Davis, the author, and Harold Ober Associates

Inc. for 'The Bones', Copyright 1959, 'Small Woman on Swallow Street', and 'Grandfather in the Old Men's Home', Copyright 1957, all from *The Drunk in the Furnace* by W. S. Merwin; for Robert Mezey to The Cummington Press and the author; for Howard Nemerov to the Margot Johnson Agency and the author; for Adrienne Rich to the author and Harper and Brothers for 'The Insusceptibles', from *The Diamond Cutters and Other Poems* by Adrienne Rich, Copyright Adrienne Rich Conrad 1955; for Louis Simpson to the author, Charles Scribner's Sons for 'The Ash and the Oak', Copyright Louis Simpson 1951, and 'Early in the Morning', Copyright Louis Simpson 1955, from POETS OF TODAY II, *Good News of Death and Other Poems* by Louis Simpson, and to Wesleyan University Press for 'To the Western World', Copyright 1957, from *A Dream of Governors* by Louis Simpson; for W. D. Snodgrass to the author and Alfred A. Knopf Inc. for poems from *Heart's Needle* by W. D. Snodgrass, Copyright 1959 W. D. Snodgrass; for Gary Snyder to Origin Press and the author; for William Stafford to the author; for Reed Whittemore to the author, the University of Minnesota Press for 'Still Life' and 'A Day with the Foreign Legion', from *An American takes a Walk and Other Poems* by Reed Whittemore, Copyright Reed Whittemore 1956, and The Macmillan Company for 'The Walk Home', 'On the Suicide of a Friend', and 'The Party', from *The Self Made Man* by Reed Whittemore, Copyright Reed Whittemore 1956, 1957, 1958, 1959; for Richard Wilbur to Faber and Faber Ltd, the author, and Harcourt, Brace and World Inc. for 'Tywater', from *The Beautiful Changes and Other Poems* by Richard Wilbur, Copyright Richard Wilbur 1947, for three poems from 'Ceremony', from *Ceremony and Other Poems* by Richard Wilbur, Copyright 1948, 1949, 1950 Richard Wilbur, and for 'After the Last Bulletins', Copyright The New Yorker Magazine Inc. 1953, from *Things of this World* by Richard Wilbur; finally, for James Wright to the author, Yale University Press for 'A Gesture by a Lady with an Assumed Name', from *The Green Wall*, and Wesleyan University Press for 'At Thomas Hardy's Birthplace, 1953', Copyright 1957, and 'Saint Judas', Copyright 1956, both from *Saint Judas* by James Wright.

# INTRODUCTION

FOR thirty years an orthodoxy ruled American poetry. It derived from the authority of T. S. Eliot and the new critics; it exerted itself through the literary quarterlies and the universities. It asked for a poetry of symmetry, intellect, irony, and wit. The last few years have broken the control of this orthodoxy. The change has come slowly and not as a rebellion of young turks against old tories. For one thing, the orthodoxy produced many good poems and some of its members are still producing them. For another, much of the attack on it came from sources – like *Time* and the publicists of the Beat Generation – which could not supply literary alternatives to the orthodoxy.

Yet we must not regret the dissolution of the old government. In modern art anarchy has proved preferable to the restrictions of a benevolent tyranny. It is preferable as a permanent condition. We do not want merely to substitute one orthodoxy for another – Down with *Understanding Poetry*! Long Live *Projective Verse*! – but we want all possibilities, even contradictory ones, to exist together. The trouble with orthodoxy is that it prescribes the thinkable limits of variation; among young poets of the forties and fifties, almost without exception, surrealism was quite literally beyond consideration. The orthodoxy which prevailed in every literary context had decided, while the poet was still in short pants, that 'surrealism had failed'. And that was the end of that. Yet typically the modern artist has allowed nothing to be beyond his consideration. He has acted as if restlessness were a conviction and has destroyed his own past in order to create a future. He has said to himself, like the policeman to the vagrant, 'Keep moving.'

Modern American poetry began in London shortly after the death of Queen Victoria. Ezra Pound recalls that Conrad Aiken told him that there was 'a guy at Harvard doing funny stuff. Mr Eliot turned up a year or so later.' Harriet Monroe founded *Poetry* in 1912, and discovered Mr Pound on her neck encouraging her to print Eliot, Frost, and Yeats. But soon after the first successes of modernist poetry in America, when Amy Lowell was flying the flag of revolution, the modernists split into opposing camps. One side of this split became the orthodoxy that prevailed from, say, 1925 to 1955.

In the first decades of this century there were the expatriates and there were the poets who remained in the United States. Pound, Aiken, and Eliot congregated in London, but things were also going on in New York. Poets and editors like Alfred Kreymbourg, Mina Loy, William Carlos Williams, Marianne Moore, Wallace Stevens, E. E. Cummings, and Hart Crane mingled and established a domestic literary milieu. They shared little but liveliness and talent, but most of them also experimented with the use of common American speech, an indigenous language increasingly distinguishable from English. Even the frenchified Wallace Stevens and the rhetorical Hart Crane participated in this endeavour. And none of these New York poets shared the concern with history which occupied Eliot and Pound, or the erudition which this concern imposed.

Pound was the link between London and Greenwich Village, as editor and publicist and even as poet. But he was unable to reconcile the slangy Williams and the polyglot Eliot. And it was the ideas of Eliot which proved attractive to the young men who took power. According to William Carlos Williams in his *Autobiography*, 'The Waste Land wiped out our world . . . Eliot returned us to the classroom.' Eliot was never further from a colloquial language than at the end of the most famous poem of our modern literature:

London bridge is falling down falling down falling down
*Poi s'ascose nel foco che gli affina*
*Quando fiam uti chelidon* – O swallow swallow
*Le Prince d'Aquitaine à la tour abolie*
These fragments I have shored against my ruins
Why then Ile fit you. Hieronymo's mad againe.
Datta. Dayadhvam. Damyata.
    Shantih shantih shantih

It was not only a matter of language, however; and in some of his poems Eliot certainly used a vocabulary and a rhythm which were close to common American speech. Eliot's attitudes towards history and tradition were more deeply relevant, as well as his sense of the continuity of American and English poetry. Probably his influence was largely accomplished through his criticism. From the mid-twenties until very recently, American poetry has functioned as a part of the English tradition. The colloquial side of American literature – the side which valued 'experience' more than 'civilization' – was neglected by the younger poets. Melville said that the whaleboats of the Pacific had been his Harvard and his Yale College; Henry James crossed the Atlantic from Harvard to Lamb House. The directions are as contrary as East and West.

The new poets admired the forms of the sixteenth and seventeenth centuries, and themselves attempted to write a symmetrical and intellectual poetry which resembled Ralegh or Dryden more than 'Gerontion' or the *Cantos*. One can divide the chief poets of this time into those who admired the tough density of Donne, and those who preferred the wit of Marvell or the delicacy of Herrick. There were Allen Tate and Yvor Winters on the one hand, and there was John Crowe Ransom on the other. Late in the thirties another group of poets took their departure most obviously from Auden – Karl Shapiro and John Frederick Nims were the best, I think – but because their poems were witty and formal they did not depart from the general area of the orthodoxy.

Immediately after the war, two books were published which were culminations of the twin strains of density and delicacy. Robert Lowell's *Lord Weary's Castle* is a monument of the line of tough rhetoricians; beyond this it was impossible to go. (The failure of John Berryman's *Homage to Mistress Bradstreet*, as I see it, only proves my point.) The effect of tremendous power under tremendous pressure was a result of a constricted subject matter and a tense line, in which the strict decasyllable was counterbalanced by eccentric caesura and violent enjambement. In contrast was Richard Wilbur's *The Beautiful Changes*, which was the peak of skilful elegance. Here was the ability to shape an analogy, to perceive and develop comparisons, to display etymological wit, and to pun six ways at once. It appealed to the mind because it was intelligent, and to the sense of form because it was intricate and shapely. It did not appeal to the passions and it did not pretend to. These two poets, though they are not the oldest here, form the real beginning of post-war American poetry because they are the culmination of past poetries.

Lowell had his imitators, but they were not very successful because Lowell's style was idiosyncratic. Many poets after Wilbur resembled him, and some of them were good at it, but the typical *ghastly* poem of the fifties was a Wilbur poem not written by Wilbur, a poem with tired wit and obvious comparisons and nothing to keep the mind or the ear occupied. (It wasn't Wilbur's fault, though I expect he will be asked to suffer for it.) The *poème bien fait*, which filled the quarterlies of the fifties, was usually not that damned *bien fait*. Too often it sounded like:

> Also the wind assumed the careful day
> And down the avenues of hollow light
> The sons of Jupiter to their dismay
> Perceived the ritual desuetude of night.

The real subject of these poems was the faint music of their diction. They were decadent products of the old move toward irony, wit, and control. The experiments of 1927 became the clichés of 1952. American poetry, which has always been outrageous – compare Whitman and Dickinson to Browning and Tennyson – dwindled into long poems in iambics called 'Herakles: A Double Sestina.' Myth, myth, myth. Jung was perhaps influential, but what distinguished these poems from the fables of Edwin Muir was that they existed in order to *prevent* meaning. Nobody could pin them down. Sometimes it seemed that the influence of Senator McCarthy was stronger than that of Jung.

Meanwhile a series of contrary directions in poetry had existed in semi-obscurity. The vanguard *New Directions* annuals printed some of them, and others survived in little mimeographed magazines and home-made pamphlets. Most of these underground poems were bad, like most poems anywhere, but they were bad in ways differing from the prevailing badness. In the thirties there was a brief upsurge of surrealism, which produced nothing. There was also a certain amount of Marxist poetry, some of it publicized, but except for the sarcasms of Kenneth Fearing little of it was readable.

The only contrary direction which endured throughout the orthodoxy was the direction I will inadequately call the colloquial, or the line of William Carlos Williams. Williams himself has been admired by most new American poets, of whatever school, but the poets of the orthodoxy have admired him for his descriptive powers; they learned from him a conscience of the eye rather than a conscience of the ear; for Williams the problem of native speech rhythm was of first importance.

This poetry is no mere restriction of one's vocabulary. It wants to use the language with the intimacy acquired in unrehearsed unliterary speech. But it has other characteristics which are not linguistic. It is a poetry of experiences more than of ideas. The experience is presented often without comment, and the words of the description must supply the emotion which the experience generates, without generalization or summary. Often too this poetry finds great pleasure in the world outside. It is the poetry of a man in the world, responding to what he sees: with disgust, with pleasure, in rant and in meditation. Naturally, this colloquial direction makes much of accuracy, of honest speech. 'Getting the tone right' is the poet's endeavour, not 'turning that metaphor neatly', or 'inventing a new stanza'. Conversely, when it fails most commonly it fails because the emotion does not sound true.

People who had learned from Williams, and from Pound's structure and metric, had a hard time of it until the fifties. Then some good editors began to print the best of them, and the movement which had lapsed in the twenties came alive again. Cid Corman started *Origin* in 1951, and printed many of the best poems written in this tradition. Jonathan Williams started the Jargon Press in North Carolina, and printed good poets who were later picked up by New York publishers. I will not try to discriminate among the various poets who belong, some quite loosely, to this strain of American literature. Denise Levertov is from England, Robert Creeley from Massachusetts, and Robert Duncan from California; the sources of their poetry are probably as varied as their geographical origins. All of these poets and many more pay tribute to an older poet named Charles Olson, who in his letters and articles and poems (though he did not begin publishing until the fifties) erected a critical standard for them. But one thing unites them all: an alternative to the traditional poetry of the last decades was necessary, and was implicit in the nature of America; a Henry James demands a Herman Melville, an English influence begets a French antagonist.

When he wrote *Life Studies*, Robert Lowell sent his muse to the *atelier* of William Carlos Williams. Many of the poets of the orthodoxy have felt the need to move on, to change. Earlier than Lowell, Richard Eberhart and Theodore Roethke moved from their original old models to new unorthodoxies. (Others, like Richard Wilbur, are staying put, and there is no reason why a man should change if he doesn't feel like changing. There is Ezra Pound but there is also Robert Frost.) I suggested that *Lord Weary's Castle* was the culmination of one movement. *Life Studies* looks like an attempt at synthesis. If the poet of rhetorical stanzas can come closer to common speech, he may avoid the mere fabrication of mandalas into available shapes. The challenge of free verse is to make shapes which derive their identity by improvisation, without reference to past poems. And also, a new form can uncover or make possible a new subject matter. Synthesis of the literary and the colloquial occurs, surely, in some of the poets of the vanguard already. An approach of the two contraries may guard against the perversions of each.

I have not mentioned another group of poets who are sufficiently separate. (I have not mentioned the Beat Generation, incidentally, because it is an invention of weekly news magazines. Insofar as it has made several good lines of poetry, it has belonged to the colloquial tradition.) These are a group of New Yorkers who have been associated with Action Painting – some have worked for *Art News*, or the Museum of Modern Art – and whose poetry attempts a similar vitality. Their closeness to modern French poetry seems obvious. Frank O'Hara, with his *Second Avenue*, comes closest to Action Writing. But the best of these poets, it seems to me, is John Ashberry, whom I print here.

Most of my comments have limited themselves to the terms of technique, like vocabulary and symmetrical form. One needs to wear certain spectacles, if one is to see everything at once. But you will notice that I repeat the eternal American tic of thinking about art in terms of its techniques.

(This tic is shared by left wing and right wing and middle.) We talk about syllabics or sestinas or a colloquial vocabulary or old spelling as if they made up a Little Marvel Poetry Kit, Free 10-Day Offer, One to a Customer, No Home Without It. The danger is that we may take technical variations more seriously than they warrant. We could argue that the movement which Robert Lowell typifies, from *Lord Weary's Castle* to *Life Studies*, is only a movement from one style of the twenties to another, from Allen Tate to William Carlos Williams, and that it is retrospective. If it makes it new, it makes it new within Lowell only.

One thing is happening in American poetry, as I see it, which is genuinely new. In lines like Robert Bly's:

> In small towns the houses are built right on the ground;
> The lamplight falls on all fours in the grass.

or Louis Simpson's:

> The clouds are lifting from the high Sierras,
> The Bay mists clearing;
> And the angel in the gate, the flowering plum,
> Dances like Italy, imagining red.

there is a kind of imagination new to American poetry. The vocabulary is mostly colloquial, but the special quality of the lines has nothing to do with an area of diction; it is a quality learned neither from T. S. Eliot nor William Carlos Williams. It is a quality closer to the spirit of Georg Trakl or Pablo Neruda, but it is not to be pigeon-holed according to any sources. This imagination is irrational, yet the poem is usually quiet and the language simple; there is no straining after apocalypse. There is an inwardness to these images, a profound subjectivity. Yet they are not subjective in the autobiographical manner of *Life Studies* or *Heart's Needle*, which are confessional and particular. Confessional poetry is certainly a widespread manner now in the United States. Snodgrass and Lowell were followed by Anne Sexton, and most effectively by Sylvia Plath in the remarkable poems she wrote before her death in 1963. Like any movement, confessional poetry has bred imitators swarming among the magazines. What began as a series of excruciating self-discoveries – often professionally aided by therapist or analyst – dissipates in an orgy of exhibitionism.

The movement which seems to me *new* is subjective but not autobiographical. It reveals through images not particular pain, but general subjective life. This universal subjective corresponds to the old objective life of shared experience and knowledge. People can talk to each other most deeply in images. To read a poem of this sort, you must not try to translate the images into abstractions. They won't go. You must try to be open to them, to let them take you over and speak in their own language of feeling. It is the intricate darkness of feeling and instinct which these poems mostly communicate. The poems are best described as expressionist: like the painter, the poet uses fantasy and distortion to express feeling. The poet may hesitate, when he is looking for a word, between opposites; would 'tiny' or 'huge' be better here?, 'mountain' or 'valley'? Such hesitation shows the irrationality and the arbitrariness of this method, but it does not imply that one of the alternatives is not enormously more appropriate than the other – only that neither is literal. The reader or the poet cannot go to the outside world and *check* – Ah, yes, the Empire State Building is 'huge' not 'tiny' – but we are not concerned with accuracy to externals; he can only make a subjective check with his inward world. When the painter hesitates between blue and green for the lady's face, he is at least certain that he will not paint it flesh-colour.

A word about making this anthology: I have made decisions about inclusions and exclusions which are highly arbitrary. I have included no poets who published books before *Lord Weary's Castle* in 1946, or who seemed to me to belong to an earlier period. The poets are arranged chronologically, *faute de mieux*; by a coincidence the oldest poet and the youngest published their first books within a year of each other. I have included only poets of whom I could print several pages, because some variety of examples seems to me necessary in a book which acts as an introduction to new poets.

*Ann Arbor, Michigan*                    DONALD HALL
*July 1961*

## *Travelling through the Dark*

TRAVELLING through the dark I found a deer
dead on the edge of the Wilson River road.
It is usually best to roll them into the canyon:
that road is narrow; to swerve might make more dead.

By glow of the tail-light I stumbled back of the car
and stood by the heap, a doe, a recent killing;
she had stiffened already, almost cold.
I dragged her off; she was large in the belly.

My fingers touching her side brought me the reason—
her side was warm; her fawn lay there waiting,
alive, still, never to be born.
Beside that mountain road I hesitated.

The car aimed ahead its lowered parking lights;
under the hood purred the steady engine.
I stood in the glare of the warm exhaust turning red;
around our group I could hear the wilderness listen.

I thought hard for us all—my only swerving—
then pushed her over the edge into the river.

## *Returned to Say*

WHEN I face north a lost Cree
on some new shore puts a moccasin down,
rock in the light and noon for seeing,
he in a hurry and I beside him.

It will be a long trip; he will be a new chief;
we have drunk new water from an unnamed stream;
under little dark trees he is to find a path
we both must travel because we have met.

Henceforth we gesture even by waiting;
there is a grain of sand on his knifeblade
so small he blows it and while his breathing
darkens the steel his eyes become set

And start a new vision: the rest of his life.
We will mean what he does. Back of this page
the path turns north. We are looking for a sign.
Our moccasins do not mark the ground.


## At Cove on the Crooked River

At Cove at our camp in the open canyon
it was the kind of place where you might look out
some evening and see trouble walking away.

And the river there meant something
always coming from snow and flashing around boulders
after shadow-fish lurking below the mesa.

We stood with wet towels over our heads for shade,
looking past the Indian picture rock and the kind of trees
that act out whatever has happened to them.

Oh civilization, I want to carve you like this,
decisively outward the way evening comes
over that kind of twist in the scenery

When people cramp into their station wagons
and roll up the windows and drive away.

## Strokes

THE left side of her world is gone –
the rest sustained by memory
and a realization: There are still the children.

Going down our porch steps her pastor
calls back: 'We are proud of her recovery,
and there is a chiropractor up in Galesburg . . .'

The birthdays of the old require such candles.


## Near

TALKING along in this not quite prose way
we all know it is not quite prose we speak,
and it is time to notice this intolerable snow
innumerably touching, before we sink.

It is time to notice, I say, the freezing snow
hesitating toward us from others' grey heaven;
listen – it is falling not quite silently
and under it still you and I are walking.

Maybe there are trumpets in the houses we pass
and a redbird watching from an evergreen –
but nothing will happen until we pause
to flame what we know, before any signal's given.

## With My Crowbar Key

I DO tricks in order to know:
careless I dance,
then turn to see
the mark to turn God left for me.

Making my home in vertigo
I pray with my screams
and think with my hair
prehensile in the dark with fear.

When I hear the well-bucket strike something soft
far down at noon,
then there's no place
far enough away to hide my face.

When I see my town over sights of a rifle,
and carved by light
from the lowering sun,
then my old friends darken one by one.

By step and step like a cat toward God
I dedicated walk,
but under the house
I realize the kitten's crouch.

And by night like this I turn and come
to this possible house
which I open, and see
myself at work with this crowbar key.

### Christmas Eve under Hooker's Statue

TONIGHT a blackout. Twenty years ago
I hung my stocking on the tree, and hell's
Serpent entwined the apple in the toe
To sting the child with knowledge. Hooker's heels
Kicking at nothing in the shifting snow,
A cannon and a cairn of cannon balls
Rusting before the blackened Statehouse, know
How the long horn of plenty broke like glass
In Hooker's gauntlets. Once I came from Mass;

Now storm-clouds shelter Christmas, once again
Mars meets his fruitless star with open arms,
His heavy sabre flashes with the rime,
The war-god's bronzed and empty forehead forms
Anonymous machinery from raw men;
The cannon on the Common cannot stun
The blundering butcher as he rides on Time –
The barrel clinks with holly. I am cold:
I ask for bread, my father gives me mould;

His stocking is full of stones. Santa in red
Is crowned with wizened berries. Man of war,
Where is the summer's garden? In its bed
The ancient speckled serpent will appear,
And black-eyed Susan with her frizzled head.
When Chancellorsville mowed down the volunteer,
'All wars are boyish,' Herman Melville said;
But we are old, our fields are running wild:
Till Christ again turn wanderer and child.

## The Holy Innocents

LISTEN, the hay-bells tinkle as the cart
Wavers on rubber tyres along the tar
And cindered ice below the burlap mill
And ale-wife run. The oxen drool and start
In wonder at the fenders of a car,
And blunder hugely up St Peter's hill.
These are the undefiled by woman – their
Sorrow is not the sorrow of this world:
King Herod shrieking vengeance at the curled-
Up knees of Jesus choking in the air,

A king of speechless clods and infants. Still
The world out-Herods Herod; and the year,
The nineteen-hundred forty-fifth of grace,
Lumbers with losses up the clinkered hill
Of our purgation; and the oxen near
The worn foundations of their resting-place,
The holy manger where their bed is corn
And holly torn for Christmas. If they die,
As Jesus, in the harness, who will mourn?
Lamb of the shepherds, Child, how still you lie.


## New Year's Day

AGAIN and then again . . . the year is born
To ice and death, and it will never do
To skulk behind storm-windows by the stove
To hear the postgirl sounding her French horn
When the thin tidal ice is wearing through.
Here is the understanding not to love
Each other, or tomorrow that will sieve
Our resolutions. While we live, we live

To snuff the smoke of victims. In the snow
The kitten heaved its hindlegs, as if fouled,
And died. We bent it in a Christmas box
And scattered blazing weeds to scare the crow
Until the snake-tailed sea-winds coughed and howled
For alms outside the church whose double locks
Wait for St Peter, the distorted key.
Under St Peter's bell the parish sea

Swells with its smelt into the burlap shack
Where Joseph plucks his hand-lines like a harp,
And hears the fearful *Puer natus est*
Of Circumcision, and relives the wrack
And howls of Jesus whom he holds. How sharp
The burden of the Law before the beast:
Time and the grindstone and the knife of God.
The Child is born in blood, O child of blood.


## Katherine's Dream

### From *Between the Porch and the Altar*

It must have been a Friday. I could hear
The top-floor typist's thunder and the beer
That you had brought in cases hurt my head;
I'd sent the pillows flying from my bed,
I hugged my knees together and I gasped.
The dangling telephone receiver rasped
Like someone in a dream who cannot stop
For breath or logic till his victim drop
To darkness and the sheets. I must have slept,
But still could hear my father who had kept
Your guilty presents but cut off my hair.
He whispers that he really doesn't care
If I am your kept woman all my life,
Or ruin your two children and your wife;

But my dishonour makes him drink. Of course
I'll tell the court the truth for his divorce.
I walk through snow into St Patrick's yard.
Black nuns with glasses smile and stand on guard
Before a bulkhead in a bank of snow,
Whose charred doors open, as good people go
Inside by twos to the confessor. One
Must have a friend to enter there, but none
Is friendless in this crowd, and the nuns smile.
I stand aside and marvel; for a while
The winter sun is pleasant and it warms
My heart with love for others, but the swarms
Of penitents have dwindled. I begin
To cry and ask God's pardon of our sin.
Where are you? You were with me and are gone.
All the forgiven couples hurry on
To dinner and their nights, and none will stop.
I run about in circles till I drop
Against a padlocked bulkhead in a yard
Where faces redden and the snow is hard.


## After the Surprising Conversions

SEPTEMBER *twenty-second*, Sir: today
I answer. In the latter part of May,
Hard on our Lord's Ascension, it began
To be more sensible. A gentleman
Of more than common understanding, strict
In morals, pious in behaviour, kicked
Against our goad. A man of some renown,
An useful, honoured person in the town,
He came of melancholy parents; prone
To secret spells, for years they kept alone –

His uncle, I believe, was killed of it:
Good people, but of too much or little wit.
I preached one Sabbath on a text from Kings;
He showed concernment for his soul. Some things
In his experience were hopeful. He
Would sit and watch the wind knocking a tree
And praise this countryside our Lord has made.
Once when a poor man's heifer died, he laid
A shilling on the doorsill; though a thirst
For loving shook him like a snake, he durst
Not entertain much hope of his estate
In heaven. Once we saw him sitting late
Behind his attic window by a light
That guttered on his Bible; through that night
He meditated terror, and he seemed
Beyond advice or reason, for he dreamed
That he was called to trumpet Judgement Day
To Concord. In the latter part of May
He cut his throat. And though the coroner
Judged him delirious, soon a noisome stir
Palsied our village. At Jehovah's nod
Satan seemed more let loose amongst us: God
Abandoned us to Satan, and he pressed
Us hard, until we thought we could not rest
Till we had done with life. Content was gone.
All the good work was quashed. We were undone.
The breath of God had carried out a planned
And sensible withdrawal from this land;
The multitude, once unconcerned with doubt,
Once neither callous, curious, nor devout,
Jumped at broad noon, as though some peddler groaned
At it in its familiar twang: 'My friend,
Cut your own throat. Cut your own throat. Now! Now!'
September twenty-second, Sir, the bough
Cracks with the unpicked apples, and at dawn
The small-mouth bass breaks water, gorged with spawn.

## Memories of West Street and Lepke

ONLY teaching on Tuesdays, book-worming
in pyjamas fresh from the washer each morning,
I hog a whole house on Boston's
'hardly passionate Marlborough Street',
where even the man
scavenging filth in the back alley trash cans,
has two children, a beach wagon, a helpmate,
and is a 'young Republican'.
I have a nine months' daughter,
young enough to be my granddaughter.
Like the sun she rises in her flame-flamingo infants' wear.

These are the tranquillized *Fifties*,
and I am forty. Ought I to regret my seedtime?
I was a fire-breathing Catholic C. O.,
and made my manic statement,
telling off the state and president, and then
sat waiting sentence in the bull pen
beside a Negro boy with curlicues
of marijuana in his hair.

Given a year,
I walked on the roof of the West Street Jail, a short
enclosure like my school soccer court,
and saw the Hudson River once a day
through sooty clothesline entanglements
and bleaching khaki tenements.
Strolling, I yammered metaphysics with Abramowitz,
a jaundice-yellow ('it's really tan')
and fly-weight pacifist,
so vegetarian,
he wore rope shoes and preferred fallen fruit.
He tried to convert Bioff and Brown,
the Hollywood pimps, to his diet.

Hairy, muscular, suburban,
wearing chocolate double-breasted suits,
they blew their tops and beat him black and blue.

I was so out of things, I'd never heard
of the Jehovah's Witnesses.
'Are you a C. O.?' I asked a fellow jailbird.
'No,' he answered, 'I'm a J. W.'
He taught me the 'hospital tuck',
and pointed out the T-shirted back
of *Murder Incorporated*'s Czar Lepke,
there piling towels on a rack,
or dawdling off to his little segregated cell full
of things forbidden the common man:
a portable radio, a dresser, two toy American
flags tied together with a ribbon of Easter palm.
Flabby, bald, lobotomized,
he drifted in a sheepish calm,
where no agonizing reappraisal
jarred his concentration on the electric chair –
hanging like an oasis in his air
of lost connexions. . . .


*For Sale*

POOR sheepish plaything,
organized with prodigal animosity,
lived in just a year –
my Father's cottage at Beverly Farms
was on the market the month he died.
Empty, open, intimate,
its town-house furniture
had an on tiptoe air
of waiting for the mover
on the heels of the undertaker.

Ready, afraid
of living alone till eighty,
Mother mooned in a window,
as if she had stayed on a train
one stop past her destination.

## Man and Wife

TAMED by *Miltown*, we lie on Mother's bed;
the rising sun in war paint dyes us red;
in broad daylight her gilded bed-posts shine,
abandoned, almost Dionysian.
At last the trees are green on Marlborough Street,
blossoms on our magnolia ignite
the morning with their murderous five days' white.
All night I've held your hand,
as if you had
a fourth time faced the kingdom of the mad —
its hackneyed speech, its homicidal eye —
and dragged me home alive. . . . Oh my *Petite*,
clearest of all God's creatures, still all air and nerve:
you were in your twenties, and I,
once hand on glass
and heart in mouth,
outdrank the Rahvs in the heat
of Greenwich Village, fainting at your feet —
too boiled and shy
and poker-faced to make a pass,
while the shrill verve
of your invective scorched the traditional South.

Now, twelve years later, you turn your back.
Sleepless, you hold
your pillow to your hollows like a child;
your old-fashioned tirade –
loving, rapid, merciless –
breaks like the Atlantic Ocean on my head.


### Skunk Hour
#### (For Elizabeth Bishop)

NAUTILUS Island's hermit
heiress still lives through winter in her Spartan cottage;
her sheep still graze above the sea.
Her son's a bishop. Her farmer
is first selectman in our village;
she's in her dotage.

Thirsting for
the hierarchic privacy
of Queen Victoria's century,
she buys up all
the eyesores facing her shore,
and lets them fall.

The season's ill –
we've lost our summer millionaire,
who seemed to leap from an L. L. Bean
catalogue. His nine-knot yawl
was auctioned off to lobstermen.
A red fox stain covers Blue Hill.

And now our fairy
decorator brightens his shop for fall;
his fishnet's filled with orange cork,
orange, his cobbler's bench and awl;
there is no money in his work,
he'd rather marry.

One dark night,
my Tudor Ford climbed the hill's skull;
I watched for love-cars. Lights turned down,
they lay together, hull to hull,
where the graveyard shelves on the town. . . .
My mind's not right.

A car radio bleats,
'Love, O careless Love. . . .' I hear
my ill-spirit sob in each blood cell,
as if my hand were at its throat. . . .
I myself am hell;
nobody's here –

only skunks, that search
in the moonlight for a bite to eat.
They march on their soles up Main Street:
white stripes, moonstruck eyes' red fire
under the chalk-dry and spar spire
of the Trinitarian Church.

I stand on top
of our back steps and breathe the rich air –
a mother skunk with her column of kittens swills the garbage
    pail.
She jabs her wedge-head in a cup
of sour cream, drops her ostrich tail,
and will not scare.

*A Poem Beginning with a Line by Pindar*

I

*THE light foot hears you and the brightness begins*
god-step at the margins of thought,
    quick adulterous tread at the heart.
Who is it that goes there?
    Where I see your quick face
notes of an old music pace the air
torso-reverberations of a Grecian lyre.

In Goya's canvas Cupid and Psyche
have a hurt voluptuous grace
bruised by redemption. The copper light
falling upon the brown boy's slight body
is carnal fate that sends the soul wailing
up from blind innocence, ensnared
    by dimness
into the deprivations of desiring sight.

But the eyes in Goya's painting are soft,
diffuse with rapture absorb the flame.
Their bodies yield out of strength.
    Waves of visual pleasure
wrap them in a sorrow previous to their impatience.

A bronze of yearning, a rose that burns
    the tips of their bodies, lips,
ends of fingers, nipples. He is not wingd.
His thighs are flesh, are clouds
    lit by the sun in its going down,
hot luminescence at the loins of the visible.

41

But they are not in a landscape.
They exist in an obscurity.

The wind spreading the sail serves them.
The two jealous sisters eager for her ruin
    serve them.
That she is ignorant, ignorant of what Love will be
    serves them,
The dark serves them.
The oil scalding his shoulder serves them,
serves their story. Fate, spinning,
    knots the threads for Love.

Jealousy, ignorance, the hurt . . . serve them.


## II

This is magic. It is passionate dispersion.
What if they grow old? The gods
    would not allow it.
    Psyche is preserved.

In time we see a tragedy, a loss of beauty
    the glittering youth
of the god retains – but from this threshold
    it is age
that is beautiful. It is toward the old poets
    we go, to their faltering,
their unaltering wrongness that has style,
    their variable truth,
    the old faces,
words shed like tears from
a plenitude of powers time stores.

A stroke.    These little strokes.    A chill.
    The old man, feeble, does not recoil.
Recall. A phase so minute,
    only a part of the word in-jerrd.

*The Thundermakers descend,*

damerging a nuv. A nerb.
   The present dented of the U
 nighted stayd.    States.    The heavy clod?
      Cloud.    Invades the brain.    What
      if lilacs last in *this* dooryard bloomd?

Hoover, Roosevelt, Truman, Eisenhower –
where among these did the power reside
that moves the heart? What flower of the nation
bride-sweet broke to the whole rapture?
Hoover, Coolidge, Harding, Wilson,
hear the factories of human misery turning out commodities.
For whom are the holy matins of the heart ringing?
Noble men in the quiet of morning hear
Indians singing the continent's violent requiem.
Harding, Wilson, Taft, Roosevelt,
idiots fumbling at the bride's door,
hear the cries of men in meaningless debt and war.
Where among these did the spirit reside
that restores the land to productive order?
McKinley, Cleveland, Harrison, Arthur,
Garfield, Hayes, Grant, Johnson,
dwell in the roots of the heart's rancour.
How sad 'amid lanes and through old woods'
   echoes Whitman's love for Lincoln!

There is no continuity then.    Only a few
   posts of the good remain.    I too
that am a nation sustain the damage
   where smokes of continual ravage
obscure the flame.
                         It is across great scars of wrong
   I reach toward the song of kindred men
   and strike again the naked string
old Whitman sang from.    Glorious mistake!
   that cried:

'The theme is creative and has vista.'
'He is the president of regulation.'

   I see always the under-side turning,
fumes that injure the tender landscape.
   From which up break
lilac blossoms of courage in daily act
   striving to meet a natural measure.


### III

*(for Charles Olson)*

          Psyche's tasks – the sorting of seeds
wheat   barley   oats   poppy   coriander
anise   beans   lentils   peas – every grain
          in its right place
                    before nightfall;

gathering the gold wool from the cannibal sheep
(for the soul must weep
   and come near upon death);

harrowing Hell for a casket Proserpina keeps
                   that must not
   be opend . . . containing beauty?

no! Melancholy coild like a serpent
                that is deadly sleep
   we are not permitted
             to succumb to.

   These are the old tasks.
   You've heard them before.

   They must be impossible. Psyche
must despair, be brought to her
               insect instructor;

must obey the counsels of the green reed;
saved from suicide by a tower speaking,
   must follow to the letter
   freakish instructions.

In the story the ants help. The old man at Pisa
   mixd in whose mind
(to draw the sorts) are all seeds
      *as a lone ant from a broken ant-hill*
had part restored by an insect, was
   upheld by a lizard

          (to draw the sorts)
*the wind is part of the process*
          defines a nation of the wind –
   father of many notions,

          Who?
let the light into the dark? began
the many movements of the passion?

            West
from east    men push.
          The islands are blessd
(cursed)    that swim below the sun,

  *man upon whom the sun has gone down!*

There is the hero who struggles east
widdershins to free the dawn    and must
          woo Night's daughter,
sorcery, black passionate rage, covetous queens,
so that the fleecy sun go    back from Troy,
   Colchis, India . . . all the blazing armies
spent, he must struggle alone toward the pyres of Day.

         The light that is Love
rushes on toward passion.    It verges upon dark.
   Roses and blood flood the clouds.
   Solitary first riders advance into legend.

This land, where I stand, was all legend
in my grandfathers' time: cattle raiders,
   animal tribes, priests, gold.
It was the West. Its vistas painters saw
   in diffuse light, in melancholy,
in abysses left by glaciers as if they had been the sun
   primordial carving empty enormities
               out of the rock.

              Snakes lurkd
guarding secrets.   Those first ones
             survived solitude.

  Scientia
holding the lamp, driven by doubt;
Eros naked in foreknowledge
smiling in his sleep;   and the light
spilld, burning his shoulder – the outrage
   that conquers legend –
passion, dismay, longing, search
   flooding up where
the Beloved is lost.   Psyche travels
life after life, my life, station
   after station,
to be tried

   without break, without
news, knowing only – but what did she know?
   The oracle at Miletus had spoken
truth surely: that he was Serpent-Desire
   that flies thru the air,
a monster-husband. But she saw him fair

whom Apollo's mouthpiece said spread
   pain
beyond cure   to those
   wounded by his arrows.

46

Rilke torn by a rose thorn
blackend toward Eros.    Cupidinous Death!
    that will not take no for an answer.


### IV

    Oh yes!    Bless the footfall where
step by step    the boundary walker
(in Maverick Road    the snow
thud by thud    from the roof
circling the house – another tread)

    that foot    informd
by the weight of all things
    that can be elusive
no more than a nearness to the mind
    of a single image

        Oh yes!    this
most dear
    the catalyst force that renders clear
the days of a life from the surrounding medium!

        Yes, beautiful rare wilderness!
wildness that verifies strength of my tame mind,
    clearing held against indians,
health that prepared to meet death,
    the stubborn hymns going up
into the ramifications of the hostile air

    that, deceptive, gives way.

Who is there?    O, light the light!
    The Indians give way,    the clearing falls.
Great Death gives way    and unprepares us.
    Lust gives way.    The Moon gives way.
Night gives way.    Minutely,    the Day gains.

She saw the body of her beloved
    dismemberd in waking . . . or was it
in sight?   *Finders Keepers* we sang
    when we were children   or were taught to sing
before our histories began   and we began
    who were beloved   our animal life
toward the Beloved,   sworn to be Keepers.


    On the hill before the wind came
the grass moved toward the one sea,
    blade after blade dancing in waves.


There the children turn the ring to the left.
There the children turn the ring to the right.
    Dancing . . . Dancing . . .


And the lonely psyche goes up thru the boy to the king
    that in the caves of history dreams.
Round and round the children turn.
    London Bridge that is a kingdom falls.


We have come so far that all the old stories
whisper once more.
Mount Segur, Mount Victoire, Mount Tamalpais . . .
    *rise to adore the mystery of Love!*


(An ode? Pindar's art, the editors tell us, was not a statue but
a mosaic, an accumulation of metaphor. But if he was archaic,
not classic, a survival of obsolete mode, there may have been
old voices in the survival that directed the heart. So, a line
from a hymn came in a novel I was reading to help me.
Psyche, poised to leap – and Pindar too, the editors write,
goes too far, topples over – listend to a tower that said
*Listen to me!* The oracle had said, *Despair! The Gods themselves abhor his power.* And then the virgin flower of the dark
falls back flesh of our flesh from which everywhere . . .

the information flows
   that is yearning. A line of Pindar
moves from the area of my lamp
   toward morning.

In the dawn that is nowhere
   I have seen the wilful children

clockwise and counter-clockwise turning.

## Still Life

I MUST explain why it is that at night, in my own house,
Even when no one's asleep, I feel I must whisper.
Thoreau and Wordsworth would call it an act of devotion,
I think; others would call it fright; it is probably
Something of both. In my living-room there are matters I'd
    rather not meddle with
Late at night.

I prefer to sit very still on the couch, watching
All the inanimate things of my daytime life –
The furniture and the curtains, the pictures and books –
Come alive,
Not as in some childish fantasy, the chairs dancing
And Disney prancing backstage, but with dignity,
The big old rocker presiding over a silent
And solemn assembly of all my craftsmen,
From Picasso and other dignities gracing my walls
To the local carpenter benched at my slippered feet.

I find these proceedings
Remarkable for their clarity and intelligence, and I wish I
    might somehow
Bring into daylight the eloquence, say, of a doorknob.
But always the gathering breaks up; everyone there
Shrinks from the tossing turbulence
Of living,
A cough, a creaking stair.

## *A Day with the Foreign Legion*

On one of those days with the Legion
When everyone sticks to sofas
And itches and bitches – a day
For gin and bitters and the plague –
Down by Mount Tessala, under the plane trees,
Seated at iron tables, cursing the country,
Cursing the times and the natives, cursing the drinks,
Cursing the food and the bugs, cursing the Legion,
Were Kim and Bim and all those brave
Heroes of all those books and plays and movies
The remorseless desert serves.
And as they sat at the iron tables cursing the country,
Cursing the food and the bugs, cursing the Legion,
Some Sergeant or other rushed in from The Fort
Gallantly bearing the news
From which all those the remorseless desert serves
Take their cues:
'Sir!'
        'What is it, Sergeant?'
                        'Sir, the hordes
March e'en now across the desert swards.'

Just like the movies.

Now in the movies
The Sergeant's arrival touches off bugles and bells,
Emptying bunks and showers, frightening horses,
Pushing up flags and standards, hardening lines
Of unsoldierly softness, and putting farewells
Hastily in the post so two weeks hence
A perfectly lovely lovely in far-off Canada
Will go pale and bite buttons and stare at the air in Canada.
And in the movies,
Almost before the audience spills its popcorn,

The company's formed and away, with Bim or Kim
Solemnly leading them out into a sandstorm,
Getting them into what is quite clearly a trap,
Posting a double guard,
Sending messengers frantic to Marrakech,
Inadvertently pouring the water away,
Losing the ammunition, horses and food,
And generally carrying on in the great tradition
By making speeches
Which bring back to mind the glorious name of the Legion,
And serve as the turning point,
After which the Arabs seem doped and perfectly helpless,
Water springs up from the ground, the horses come back,
Plenty of food is discovered in some old cave,
And reinforcements arrive led by the girl
From Canada.

But in this instance nothing from *Beau Geste*
Or the Paramount lot was attempted,
It being too hot, too terribly hot, for dramatics
Even from Kim and Bim
Aging under the plane trees,
Cursing the food and the bugs, cursing the Sergeant
Who gallantly bore the news because he was young,
Full of oats and ignorance, so damned young
In his pretty khaki; nothing at all,
So late in the day, with everyone crocked
And bitten to death and sweaty and all,
Was attempted despite the Sergeant,
Who whirled on his heel, his mission accomplished, and
    marched,
Hip hip,
Out of the bar, a true trooper, as if to the wars.

So the lights went on and the audience,
Pleasantly stupid, whistled and clapped at the rarity
Of a film breaking down in this late year of Our Lord.

But of course it was not the film; it was not the projector;
Nor was it the man in the booth, who hastened away
As soon as the feature was over, leaving the heroes
Cursing the food and the bugs, cursing the Legion
As heathendom marched and the Sergeant whirled, hip hip;
But some other, darker cause having to do
With the script perhaps, or the art.
Or not art –
None of these but still deeper, deeper and darker,
Rooted in Culture or . . . Culture, or . . .

Or none of these things. Or all.

What was it?

None of these things, or all. It was the time,
The time and the place, and how could one blame them,
Seated at iron tables cursing the country?
What could they do,
Seated under the plane trees watching the Sergeant
Whirl on his heel, hip hip, in his pretty khaki?
What could they say,
Drinking their gin and bitters by Mount Tessala,
What could they say?

For what after all *could* be said,
After all was said,
But that the feature had merely run out, and the lights had
    gone on
Because it was time for the lights to go on, and time
For them not to dash out in the desert,
But to rage
As befitted their age
At the drinks and the country, letting their audience
Clap, stamp, whistle and hoot as darkness
Settled on Mount Tessala, the lights went on,
The enemy roamed the desert, and everyone itched.

## On the Suicide of a Friend

SOME there are who are present at such occasions,
And conduct themselves with appropriate feeling and grace.
But they are the rare ones. Mostly the friends and relations
Are caught playing cards or eating miles from the place.
What happens on that dark river, or road, or mountain
Passes unnoticed as friend trumps loved one's ace.
Perhaps he knew this about them – worse, he did not,
And raged over the brink of that road or mountain
Thinking at least they'd remember before they forgot.
Either way, now he is dead and done with that lot.

## The Party

THEY served tea in the sandpile, together with
Mudpies baked on the sidewalk.
After tea
The youngest said that he had had a good dinner,
The oldest dressed for a dance,
And they sallied forth together with watering pots
To moisten a rusted fire truck on account of it
Might rain.

I watched from my study,
Thought of my part in these contributions to world
Gaiety, and resolved
That the very least acknowledgement I could make
Would be to join them;
                              so we
All took our watering pots (filled with pies)
And poured tea on our dog. Then I kissed the children
And told them that when they grew up we would have
Real tea parties.
'That did be fun!' the youngest shouted, and ate pies
With wild surmise.

## The Walk Home

As one grows older and Caesar, Hitler,
Lear, and the salesman are bundled off one by one,
It is hard to sustain discomposure. The files thicken.
'Leaves,' says the poet, 'grass, and birds of the field,'
Conjuring up a glass and a good book
On some green hill
Where nobody bears or cares more than old care will.

Who's in, who's out — such words harden
In bronze or plastic; pipes and slippers
Move to their destined places, swords to theirs;
And one walking home at dusk with the evening paper
Thinks with erosive irreverence that perhaps
He should let his subscription to that sheet lapse.

What, then, would the world do? As swords clashed
Under the sun, and Prince Hal and Sir Winston
Triumphed on all continents, would then the word
Sweep the ranks that one watching watched no longer?
As he closed his eyes to all but his own thin theme,
Would the world then oblige, age and dream his dream?

Dream. Dream. And still dream. And leave not a wrack.
As one grows older
Plato's, Bottom's and all such country rouses
Thicken the files with the rest;
And walking home at dusk with the sages, age
Thinks no more than age must always think:—
The world doesn't oblige, and old pipes stink.

## Storm Windows

PEOPLE are putting up storm windows now,
Or were, this morning, until the heavy rain
Drove them indoors. So, coming home at noon,
I saw storm windows lying on the ground,
Frame-full of rain; through the water and glass
I saw the crushed grass, how it seemed to stream
Away in lines like seaweed on the tide
Or blades of wheat leaning under the wind.
The ripple and splash of rain on the blurred glass
Seemed that it briefly said, as I walked by,
Something I should have liked to say to you,
Something . . . the dry grass bent under the pane
Brimful of bouncing water . . . something of
A swaying clarity which blindly echoes
This lonely afternoon of memories
And missed desires, while the wintry rain
(Unspeakable, the distance in the mind!)
Runs on the standing windows and away.

## The Statues in the Public Gardens

ALONE at the end of green *allées*, alone
Where a path turns back upon itself, or else
Where several paths converge, green bronze, grey stone,
The weatherbeaten famous figures wait
Inside their basins, on their pedestals,
Till time, as promised them, wears out of date.

Around them rise the willow, birch, and elm,
Sweet shaken pliancies in the weather now.

The granite hand is steady on the helm,
The sword, the pen, unshaken in the hand,
The bandage and the laurel on the brow:
The last obedience is the last command.

Children and nurses eddying through the day,
Old gentlemen with newspapers and canes,
And licit lovers, public as a play,
Never acknowledge the high regard of fame
Across their heads – the patriot's glare, the pains
Of prose – and scarcely stop to read a name.

Children, to be illustrious is sad.
Do not look up. Those empty eyes are stars,
Their glance the constellation of the mad
Who must be turned to stone. To save your garden,
My playful ones, these pallid voyagers
Stand in the streak of rain, imploring pardon.

At night the other lovers come to play
Endangered games, and robbers lie in wait
To knock old ladies with a rock; but they
Tremble to come upon these stony men
And suffragettes, who shine like final fate
In the electric green of every glen.

For it is then that statues suffer their
Sacrificed lives, and sigh through fruitless trees
After the flesh. Their sighs tremble the air,
They would surrender sceptres, swords, and globes,
Feeling the soft flank shudder to the breeze
Under the greatcoats and the noble robes.

In darker glades, the nearly naked stone
Of athlete, goddess chaste as any snows
That stain them winters, tempts maiden and man
From their prosthetic immortality:
Pythagoras' thigh, or Tycho's golden nose,
For a figleaf fallen from the withered tree.

## A Singular Metamorphosis

WE all were watching the quiz on television
Last night, combining leisure with pleasure,
When Uncle Henry's antique *escritoire*,
Where he used to sit making up his accounts,
Began to shudder and rock like a crying woman,
Then burst into flower from every cubbyhole
(For all the world like a seventy-four of the line
Riding the swell and firing off Finisterre).
Extraordinary sight! Its delicate legs
Thickened and gnarled, writhing, they started to root
The feet deep in a carpet of briony
Star-pointed with primula. Small animals
Began to mooch around and climb up this
Reversionary desk and dustable heirloom
Left in the gloomiest corner of the room
Far from the television.

                              I alone,
To my belief, remarked the remarkable
Transaction above remarked. The flowers were blue,
The fiery blue of iris, and there was
A smell of warm, wet grass and new horse-dung.

The screen, meanwhile, communicated to us
With some fidelity the image and voice
Of Narcisse, the cultivated policewoman
From San Francisco, who had already
Taken the sponsors for ten thousand greens
By knowing her Montalets from Capegues,
Cordilleras from Gonorrheas, in
The Plays of Shapesmoke Swoon of Avalon,
A tygers hart in a players painted hide
If ever you saw one.

                              When all this was over,
And everyone went home to bed, not one

Mentioned the *escritoire*, which was by now
Bowed over with a weight of fruit and nuts
And birds and squirrels in its upper limbs.
Stars tangled with its mistletoe and ivy.

## The View from an Attic Window
### (For Francis and Barbara)

I

AMONG the high-branching, leafless boughs
Above the roof-peaks of the town,
Snowflakes unnumberably come down.

I watched out of the attic window
The laced sway of family trees,
Intricate genealogies

Whose strict, reserved gentility,
Trembling, impossible to bow,
Received the appalling fall of snow.

All during Sunday afternoon,
Not storming, but befittingly,
Out of a still, grey, devout sky,

The snowflakes fell, until all shapes
Went under, and thickening, drunken lines
Cobwebbed the sleep of solemn pines.

Up in the attic, among many things
Inherited and out of style,
I cried, then fell asleep awhile,

Waking at night now, as the snowflakes from darkness to darkness go
Past yellow lights in the street below.

II

I cried because life is hopeless and beautiful.
And like a child I cried myself to sleep
High in the head of the house, feeling the hull
Beneath me pitch and roll among the steep
Mountains and valleys of the many years
    Which brought me to tears.

Down in the cellar, furnace and washing machine,
Pump, fuse-box, water-heater, work their hearts
Out at my life, which narrowly runs between
Them and this cemetery of spare parts
For discontinued men, whose hats and canes
    Are my rich remains.

And women, their portraits and wedding gowns
Stacked in the corners, brooding in wooden trunks;
And children's rattles, books about lions and clowns;
And headless, hanging dresses sway like drunks
Whenever a living footstep shakes the floor;
    I mention no more;

But what I thought today, that made me cry,
Is this, that we live in two kinds of thing:
The powerful trees, thrusting into the sky
Their black patience, are one, and that branching
Relation teaches how we endure and grow;
    The other is the snow,

Falling in a white chaos from the sky,
As many as the sands of all the seas,
As all the men who died or who will die,
As stars in heaven, as leaves of all the trees;
As Abraham was promised of his seed;
    Generations bleed,

Till I, high in the tower of my time
Among familiar ruins, began to cry
For accident, sickness, justice, war and crime,
Because all died, because I had to die.
The snow fell, the trees stood, the promise kept,
   And a child I slept.


## The Fall Again

IT is the Old Man through the sleeping town
Comes oil-dark to a certain lip, and breaks
By the white rain's beard the word he speaks,
A drunken Babel that stuns on a stone
And leaps in shatterings of light against
Its pouring fall, and falls again to spill
Asleep its darkening strength along the kill
On those great sinews' curves twisted and tensed.
Between the vineyard and the drunken dark,
O sorrow, there the rainbow shines no more,
There promises are broken in the roar
Of that Old Man, the staggered Patriarch
And whitebeard falling naked to the floor
Ashamed, who was himself both Flood and Ark.

### Tywater

DEATH of Sir Nihil, book the *n*th,
Upon the charred and clotted sward,
Lacking the lily of our Lord,
Alases of the hyacinth.

Could flicker from behind his ear
A whistling silver throwing knife
And with a holler punch the life
Out of a swallow in the air.

Behind the lariat's butterfly
Shuttled his white and gritted grin,
And cuts of sky would roll within
The noose-hole, when he spun it high.

The violent, neat and practised skill
Was all he loved and all he learned;
When he was hit, his body turned
To clumsy dirt before it fell.

And what to say of him, God knows.
Such violence. And such repose.

## 'A World Without Objects is a Sensible Emptiness'

THE tall camels of the spirit
Steer for their deserts, passing the last groves loud
With the sawmill shrill of the locust, to the whole honey of
    the arid
    Sun. They are slow, proud,

And move with a stilted stride
To the land of sheer horizon, hunting Traherne's
*Sensible emptiness*, there where the brain's lantern-slide
    Revels in vast returns.

O connoisseurs of thirst,
Beasts of my soul who long to learn to drink
Of pure mirage, those prosperous islands are accurst
    That shimmer on the brink

Of absence; auras, lustres,
And all shinings need to be shaped and borne.
Think of those painted saints, capped by the early masters
    With bright, jauntily-worn

Aureate plates, or even
Merry-go-round rings. Turn, O turn
From the fine sleights of the sand, from the long empty oven
    Where flames in flamings burn

Back to the trees arrayed
In bursts of glare, to the halo-dialling run
Of the country creeks, and the hills' bracken tiaras made
    Gold in the sunken sun,

Wisely watch for the sight
Of the supernova burgeoning over the barn,
Lampshine blurred in the steam of beasts, the spirit's right
    Oasis, light incarnate.

## Museum Piece

THE good grey guardians of art
Patrol the halls on spongy shoes,
Impartially protective, though
Perhaps suspicious of Toulouse.

Here dozes one against the wall,
Disposed upon a funeral chair.
A Degas dancer pirouettes
Upon the parting of his hair.

See how she spins! The grace is there,
But strain as well is plain to see.
Degas loved the two together:
Beauty joined to energy.

Edgar Degas purchased once
A fine El Greco, which he kept
Against the wall beside his bed
To hang his pants on while he slept.


## After the Last Bulletins

AFTER the last bulletins the windows darken
And the whole city founders readily and deep,
Sliding on all its pillows
To the thronged Atlantis of personal sleep,

And the wind rises. The wind rises and bowls
The day's litter of news in the alleys. Trash
Tears itself on the railings,
Soars and falls with a soft crash,

Tumbles and soars again. Unruly flights
Scamper the park, and taking a statue for dead
Strike at the positive eyes,
Batter and flap the stolid head

And scratch the noble name. In empty lots
Our journals spiral in a fierce noyade
Of all we thought to think,
Or caught in corners cramp and wad

And twist our words. And some from gutters flail
Their tatters at the tired patrolman's feet,
Like all that fisted snow
That cried beside his long retreat

Damn you! damn you! to the emperor's horse's heels.
Oh none too soon through the air white and dry
Will the clear announcer's voice
Beat like a dove, and you and I

From the heart's anarch and responsible town
Return by subway-mouth to life again,
Bearing the morning papers,
And cross the park where saintlike men

White and absorbed, with stick and bag remove
The litter of the night, and footsteps rouse
With confident morning sound
The songbirds in the public boughs.

## She

WHAT was her beauty in our first estate
When Adam's will was whole, and the least thing
Appeared the gift and creature of his king,
How should we guess? Resemblance had to wait

For separation, and in such a place
She so partook of water, light, and trees
As not to look like any one of these.
He woke and gazed into her naked face.

But then she changed, and coming down amid
The flocks of Abel and the fields of Cain,
Clothed in their wish, her Eden graces hid,
A shape of plenty with a mop of grain,

She broke upon the world, in time took on
The look of every labour and its fruits.
Columnar in a robe of pleated lawn
She cupped her patient hand for attributes,

Was radiant captive of the farthest tower
And shed her honour on the fields of war,
Walked in her garden at the evening hour,
Her shadow like a dark ogival door,

Breasted the seas for all the westward ships
And, come to virgin empires, changed again –
A moonlike being truest in eclipse
And subject goddess of the dreams of men.

Tree, temple, valley, prow, gazelle, machine,
More named and nameless than the morning star,
Lovely in every shape, in all unseen,
We dare not wish to find you as you are,

Whose apparition, biding time until
Desire decay and bring the latter age,
Shall flourish in the ruins of our will
And deck the broken stones like saxifrage.

## The Undead

EVEN as children they were late sleepers,
Preferring their dreams, even when quick with monsters,
    To the world with all its breakable toys,
        Its compacts with the dying;

From the stretched arms of withered trees
'They turned, fearing contagion of the mortal,
    And even under the plums of summer
        Drifted like winter moons.

Secret, unfriendly, pale, possessed
Of the one wish, the thirst for mere survival,
    They came, as all extremists do
        In time, to a sort of grandeur:

Now, to their Balkan battlements
Above the vulgar town of their first lives,
    They rise at the moon's rising. Strange
        That their utter self-concern

Should, in the end, have left them selfless:
Mirrors fail to perceive them as they float
    Through the great hall and up the staircase;
        Nor are the cobwebs broken.

Into the pallid night emerging,
Wrapped in their flapping capes, routinely maddened
    By a wolf's cry, they stand for a moment
        Stoking the mind's eye

With lewd thoughts of the pressed flowers
And bric-à-brac of rooms with something to lose,–
　　Of love-dismembered dolls, and children
　　　　Buried in quilted sleep.

Then they are off in a negative frenzy,
Their black shapes cropped into sudden bats
　　That swarm, burst, and are gone. Thinking
　　　　Of a thrush cold in the leaves

Who has sung his few summers truly,
Or an old scholar resting his eyes at last,
　　We cannot be much impressed with vampires,
　　　　Colourful though they are;

Nevertheless, their pain is real,
And requires our pity. Think how sad it must be
　　To thirst always for a scorned elixir,
　　　　The salt quotidian blood

Which, if mistrusted, has no savour;
To prey on life forever and not possess it,
　　As rock-hollows, tide after tide,
　　　　Glassily strand the sea.


## In the Smoking Car

THE eyelids meet. He'll catch a little nap.
The grizzled, crew-cut head drops to his chest.
It shakes above the briefcase on his lap.
Close voices breathe, 'Poor sweet, he did his best.'

'Poor sweet, poor sweet,' the bird-hushed glades repeat,
Through which in quiet pomp his litter goes,
Carried by native girls with naked feet.
A sighing stream concurs in his repose.

Could he but think, he might recall to mind
The righteous mutiny or sudden gale
That beached him here; the dear ones left behind . . .
So near the ending, he forgets the tale.

Were he to lift his eyelids now, he might
Behold his maiden porters, brown and bare.
But even here he has no appetite.
It is enough to know that they are there.

Enough that now a honeyed music swells,
The gentle, mossed declivities begin,
And the whole air is full of flower-smells.
Failure, the longed-for valley, takes him in.

## Shame

IT is a cramped little state with no foreign policy,
Save to be thought inoffensive. The grammar of the language
Has never been fathomed, owing to the national habit
Of allowing each sentence to trail off in confusion.
Those who have visited Scusi, the capital city,
Report that the railway-route from Schuldig passes
Through country best described as unrelieved.
Sheep are the national product. The faint inscription
Over the city gates may perhaps be rendered,
'I'm afraid you won't find much of interest here.'
Census-reports which give the population
As zero are, of course, not to be trusted,
Save as reflecting the natives' flustered insistence
That they do not count, as well as their modest horror
Of letting one's sex be known in so many words.
The uniform grey of the nondescript buildings, the absence
Of churches or comfort-stations, have given observers
An odd impression of ostentatious meanness,

And it must be said of the citizens (muttering by
In their ratty sheepskins, shying at cracks in the sidewalk)
That they lack the peace of mind of the truly humble.
The tenor of life is careful, even in the stiff
Unsmiling carelessness of the border-guards
And *douaniers*, who admit, whenever they can,
Not merely the usual carloads of deodorant
But gypsies, g-strings, hasheesh, and contraband pigments.
Their complete negligence is reserved, however,
For the hoped-for invasion, at which time the happy people
(Sniggering, ruddily naked, and shamelessly drunk)
Will stun the foe by their overwhelming submission,
Corrupt the generals, infiltrate the staff,
Usurp the throne, proclaim themselves to be sun-gods,
And bring about the collapse of the whole empire.

# ANTHONY HECHT

## Alceste in the Wilderness

*Non, je ne puis souffrir cette lâche méthode*
*Qu'affectent la plupart de vos gens à la mode . . .*
                    MOLIÈRE, *Le Misanthrope*

EVENING is clogged with gnats as the light fails,
And branches bloom with gold and copper screams
Of birds with figured and sought-after tails
To plume a lady's gear; the motet wails
Through Africa upon dissimilar themes.

A little snuffbox whereon Daphnis sings
In pale enamels, touching love's defeat,
Calls up the colour of her underthings
And plays upon the taut memorial strings,
Trailing her laces down into this heat.

One day he found, topped with a smutty grin,
The small corpse of a monkey, partly eaten.
Force of the sun had split the bluish skin,
Which, by their questioning and entering in,
A swarm of bees had been concerned to sweeten.

He could distill no essence out of this.
That yellow majesty and molten light
Should bless this carcass with a sticky kiss
Argued a brute and filthy emphasis.
The half-moons of the fingernails were white,

And where the nostrils opened on the skies,
Issuing to the sinus, where the ant
Crawled swiftly down to undermine the eyes
Of cloudy aspic, nothing could disguise
How terribly the thing looked like Philinte.

Will-o'-the-wisp, on the scum-laden water,
Burns in the night, a gaseous deceiver,
In the pale shade of France's foremost daughter.
Heat gives his thinking cavity no quarter,
For he is burning with the monkey's fever.

Before the bees have diagrammed their comb
Within the skull, before summer has cracked
The back of Daphnis, naked, polychrome,
Versailles shall see the tempered exile home,
Peruked and stately for the final act.

## Samuel Sewall

SAMUEL SEWALL, in a world of wigs,
Flouted opinion in his personal hair;
For foppery he gave not any figs,
But in his right and honour took the air.

Thus in his naked style, though well attired,
He went forth in the city, or paid court
To Madam Winthrop, whom he much admired,
Most godly, but yet liberal with the port.

And all the town admired for two full years
His excellent address, his gifts of fruit,
Her gracious ways and delicate white ears,
And held the course of nature absolute.

But yet she bade him suffer a peruke,
'That One be not distinguished from the All';
Delivered of herself this stern rebuke
Framed in the resonant language of St Paul.

'Madam,' he answered her, 'I have a Friend
Furnishes me with hair out of His strength,
And He requires only I attend
Unto His charity and to its length.'

And all the town was witness to his trust:
On Monday he walked out with the Widow Gibbs,
A pious lady of charm and notable bust,
Whose heart beat tolerably beneath her ribs.

On Saturday he wrote proposing marriage,
And closed, imploring that she be not cruel,
'Your favourable answer will oblige,
Madam, your humble servant, Samuel Sewall.'

## The Vow

IN the third month, a sudden flow of blood.
The mirth of tabrets ceaseth, and the joy
Also of the harp. The frail image of God
Lay spilled and formless. Neither girl nor boy,
But yet blood of my blood, nearly my child.
   All that long day
Her pale face turned to the window's mild
   Featureless grey.

And for some nights she whimpered as she dreamed
The dead thing spoke, saying: 'Do not recall
Pleasure at my conception. I am redeemed
From pain and sorrow. Mourn rather for all
Who breathlessly issue from the bone gates,
   The gates of horn,
For truly it is best of all the fates
   Not to be born.

'Mother, a child lay gasping for bare breath
On Christmas Eve when Santa Claus had set
Death in the stocking, and the lights of death
Flamed in the tree. O, if you can, forget
You were the child, turn to my father's lips
   Against the time
When his cold hand puts forth its fingertips
   Of jointed lime.'

Doctors of Science, what is man that he
Should hope to come to a good end? *The best
Is not to have been born.* And could it be
That Jewish diligence and Irish jest
The consent of flesh and a midwinter storm
    Had reconciled,
Was yet too bold a mixture to inform
    A simple child?

Even as gold is tried, Gentile and Jew.
If that ghost was a girl's, I swear to it:
Your mother shall be far more blessed than you.
And if a boy's, I swear: The flames are lit
That shall refine us; they shall not destroy
    A living hair.
Your younger brothers shall confirm in joy
    This that I swear.

## *The End of the Weekend*

A DYING firelight slides along the quirt
Of the cast-iron cowboy where he leans
Against my father's books. The lariat
Whirls into darkness. My girl, in skin-tight jeans,
Fingers a page of Captain Marryat,
Inviting insolent shadows to her shirt.

We rise together to the second floor.
Outside, across the lake, an endless wind
Whips at the headstones of the dead and wails
In the trees for all who have and have not sinned.
She rubs against me and I feel her nails.
Although we are alone, I lock the door.

The eventual shapes of all our formless prayers,
This dark, this cabin of loose imaginings,
Wind, lake, lip, everything awaits
The slow unloosening of her underthings.
And then the noise. Something is dropped. It grates
Against the attic beams.
                I climb the stairs
Armed with a belt.
              A long magnesium strip
Of moonlight from the dormer cuts a path
Among the shattered skeletons of mice.
A great black presence beats its wings in wrath.
Above the boneyard burn its golden eyes.
Some small grey fur is pulsing in its grip.

### 'More Light! More Light!'

COMPOSED in the Tower before his execution
These moving verses, and being brought at that time
Painfully to the stake, submitted, declaring thus:
'I implore my God to witness that I have made no crime.'

Nor was he forsaken of courage, but the death was horrible,
The sack of gunpowder failing to ignite.
His legs were blistered sticks on which the black sap
Bubbled and burst as he howled for the Kindly Light.

And that was but one, and by no means one of the worst;
Permitted at least his pitiful dignity;
And such as were by made prayers in the name of Christ,
That shall judge all men, for his soul's tranquillity.

We move now to outside a German wood.
Three men are there commanded to dig a hole
In which the two Jews are ordered to lie down
And be buried alive by the third, who is a Pole.

Not light from the shrine at Weimar beyond the hill
Nor light from heaven appeared. But he did refuse.
A Lüger settled back deeply in its glove.
He was ordered to change places with the Jews.

Much casual death had drained away their souls.
The thick dirt mounted toward the quivering chin.
When only the head was exposed the order came
To dig him out again and to get back in.

No light, no light in the blue Polish eye.
When he finished a riding boot packed down the earth.
The Lüger hovered lightly in its glove.
He was shot in the belly and in three hours bled to death.

No prayers or incense rose up in those hours
Which grew to be years, and every day came mute
Thousands sifting down through the crisp air
And settled upon his eyes in a black soot.

## The Performance

THE last time I saw Donald Armstrong
He was staggering oddly off into the sun,
Going down, of the Philippine Islands.
I let my shovel fall, and put that hand
Above my eyes, and moved some way to one side
That his body might pass through the sun,

And I saw how well he was not
Standing there on his hands,
On his spindle-shanked forearms balanced,
Unbalanced, with his big feet looming and waving
In the great, untrustworthy air
He flew in each night, when it darkened.

Dust fanned in scraped puffs from the earth
Between his arms, and blood turned his face inside out,
To demonstrate its suppleness
Of veins, as he perfected his role.
Next day, he toppled his head off
On an island beach to the south,

And the enemy's two-handed sword
Did not fall from anyone's hands
At that miraculous sight,
As the head rolled over upon
Its wide-eyed face, and fell
Into the inadequate grave

He had dug for himself, under pressure.
Yet I put my flat hand to my eyebrows
Months later, to see him again

In the sun, when I learned how he died,
And imagined him, there,
Come, judged, before his small captors,

Doing all his lean tricks to amaze them —
The back somersault, the kip-up —
And at last, the stand on his hands,
Perfect, with his feet together,
His head down, evenly breathing,
As the sun poured up from the sea

And the headsman broke down
In a blaze of tears, in that light
Of the thin, long human frame
Upside down in its own strange joy,
And, if some other one had not told him,
Would have cut off the feet

Instead of the head,
And if Armstrong had not presently risen
In kingly, round-shouldered attendance,
And then knelt down in himself
Beside his hacked, glittering grave, having done
All things in this life that he could.


### Hunting Civil War Relics at
### Nimblewill Creek

As he moves the mine-detector
A few inches over the ground,
Making it vitally float
Among the ferns and weeds,
I come into this war
Slowly, with my one brother,
Watching his face grow deep
Between the earphones,

For I can tell
If we enter the buried battle
Of Nimblewill
Only by his expression.

Softly he wanders, parting
The grass with a dreaming hand.
No dead cry yet takes root
In his clapped ears
Or can be seen in his smile.
But underfoot I feel
The dead regroup,
The burst metals all in place,
The battle lines be drawn
Anew to include us
In Nimblewill,
And I carry the shovel and pick

More as if they were
Bright weapons that I bore.
A bird's cry breaks
In two, and into three parts.
We cross the creek; the cry
Shifts into another,
Nearer, bird, and is
Like the shout of a shadow —
Lived-with, appallingly close —
Or the soul, pronouncing
'Nimblewill':
Three tones; your being changes.

We climb the bank;
A faint light glows
On my brother's mouth.
I listen, as two birds fight
For a single voice, but he
Must be hearing the grave.

In pieces, all singing
To his clamped head,
For he smiles as if
He rose from the dead within .
Green Nimblewill
And stood in his grandson's shape.

No shot from the buried war
Can kill me now,
For the dead have waited here
A hundred years to create
The look on a man's loved features,
While I stand, with
The same voice calling insanely
Like that of a sniper
Who throws down his rifle and yells
In the pure joy of missing me
At Nimblewill
And my brother beside me holds

A long-buried light on his lips.
I fall to my knees
To dig wherever he points,
To bring up mess-tin or bullet,
To go underground
Still singing, myself,
Like a hidden bird,
Or a man who renounces war,
Or one who shall lift up the past,
Not breathing 'Father,'
At Nimblewill,
But saying, 'Fathers! Fathers!'

## Overland to the Islands

LET's go – much as that dog goes,
intently haphazard. The
Mexican light on a day that
'smells like autumn in Connecticut'
makes iris ripples on his
black gleaming fur – and that too
is as one would desire – a radiance
consorting with the dance.
                       Under his feet
rocks and mud, his imagination, sniffing,
engaged in its perceptions – dancing
edgeways, there's nothing
the dog disdains on his way,
nevertheless he
keeps moving, changing
pace and approach but
not direction – 'every step an arrival'.

## Sunday Afternoon

AFTER the First Communion
and the banquet of mangoes and
bridal cake, the young daughters
of the coffee merchant lay down
for a long siesta, and their white dresses
lay beside them in quietness
and the white veils floated
In their dreams as the flies buzzed.

But as the afternoon
burned to a close they rose
and ran about the neighbourhood
among the halfbuilt villas
alive, alive, kicking a basketball, wearing
other new dresses, of bloodred velvet.


### The Springtime

THE red eyes of rabbits
aren't sad. No one passes
the sad golden village in a barge
any more. The sunset
will leave it alone. If the
curtains hang askew
it is no one's fault.
Around and around and around
everywhere the same sound
of wheels going, and things
growing older, growing
silent. If the dogs
bark to each other
all night, and their eyes
flash red, that's
nobody's business. They have
a great space of dark to
bark across. The rabbits
will bare their teeth at
the spring moon.

## The Grace-note

I N Sabbath quiet, a street
of closed warehouses and wholesale silence,
Adam Misery, while the cop frisks him

lifts with both hands his lip and
drooping moustache to reveal
horse-teeth for inspection.

                Nothing
is new to him and he is not afraid.
This is a world. As the artist

extends his world with
one gratuitous flourish – a stroke of white or
a run on the clarinet above the

base tones of the orchestra – so he
ornaments his with
fresh contempt.

## The World Outside

### I

O N the kitchen wall a flash
of shadow:
           swift pilgrimage
of pigeons, a spiral
celebration of air, of sky-deserts.
And on tenement windows
a blaze
       of lustred watermelon:
stain of the sun
westering somewhere back of Hoboken.

## II

The goatherd upstairs! Music
from his sweet flute
roves from summer to summer
in the dusty air of airshafts
and among the flakes
of soot that float
in a daze from chimney
to chimney – notes
remote, cool, speaking of slender
shadows under olive-leaves. A silence.

## III

Groans, sighs, in profusion,
with coughing, muttering, orchestrate
solitary grief; the crash of glass, a low voice
repeating over and over, 'No.
    No. I want my key. No you did not.
    No.' – a commonplace.
And in counterpoint, from other windows,
the effort to be merry – ay, maracas!
– sibilant, intricate – the voices wailing pleasure,
    arriving perhaps at joy, late, after sets
have been switched off, and silences
are dark windows?

## Six Variations

### I

WE have been shown
how Basket drank –
and old man Volpe the cobbler
made up what words he didn't know
so that his own son, even,
laughed at him: but with respect.

II

Two flutes! How close
to each other they move
in mazing figures,
never touching, never
breaking the measure,
as gnats dance in
summer haze all afternoon, over
shallow water sprinkled
with mottled blades of willow—
two flutes!

III

Shlup, shlup, the dog
as it laps up
water
makes intelligent
music, resting
now and then to
take breath in irregular
measure.

IV

When I can't
strike one spark from you,
when you don't
look me in the eye,
when your answers
come
          slowly, dragging
their feet, and furrows
change your face,
when the sky is a cellar
with dirty windows,
when furniture
obstructs the body, and bodies

are heavy furniture coated
with dust – time
for a lagging leaden pace,
a short sullen line,
measure
of heavy heart and
cold eye.

V

The quick of the sun that gilds
broken pebbles in sidewalk cement
and the iridescent
spit, that defiles and adorns!
Gold light in blind love does not distinguish
one surface from another, the savour
is the same to its tongue, the fluted
cylinder of a new ashcan a dazzling silver,
the smooth flesh of screaming children a
        quietness, it is all
a jubilance, the light catches up
the disordered street in its apron,
broken fruitrinds shine in the gutter.

VI

Lap up the vowels
of sorrow,
                transparent, cold
water-darkness welling
up from the white sand.
Hone the blade
of a scythe to cut swathes
of light sound in the mind.
Through the hollow globe, a ring
of frayed rusty scrapiron,
is it the sea that shines?
Is it a road at the world's edge?

## A Map of the Western Part of the County of Essex in England

SOMETHING forgotten twenty years: though my fathers
and mothers came from Cordova and Vitepsk and Caer-
 narvon,
and though I am a citizen of the United States and less a
stranger here than anywhere else, perhaps,
I am Essex-born:
Cranbrook Wash called me into its dark tunnel,
the little streams of Valentines heard my resolves,
Roding held my head above water when I thought it was
drowning me; in Hainault only a haze of thin trees
stood between the red doubledecker buses and the boar-
 hunt,
the spirit of merciful Phillippa glimmered there.
Pergo Park knew me, and Clavering, and Havering-atte-
 Bower,
Stanford Rivers lost me in osier-beds, Stapleford Abbots
sent me safe home on the dark road after Simeon-quiet
 evensong,
Wanstead drew me over and over into its basic poetry,
in its serpentine lake I saw bass-viols among the golden dead
 leaves,
through its trees the ghost of a great house. In
Ilford High Road I saw the multitudes passing pale under
 the
light of flaring sundown, seven kings
in sombre starry robes gathered at Seven Kings
the place of law
where my birth and marriage are recorded
and the death of my father. Woodford Wells
where an old house was named The Naked Beauty (a white
statue forlorn in its garden)
saw the meeting and parting of two sisters
(forgotten? and further away

87

the hill before Thaxted? where peace befell us? not once
but many times?)
All the Ivans dreaming of their villages
all the Marias dreaming of their walled cities,
picking up fragments of New World slowly
not knowing how to put them together nor how to join
image with image, now I know how it was with you, an old
   map
made long before I was born shows ancient
rights of way where I walked when I was ten burning with
   desire
for the world's great splendours, a child who traced voyages
indelibly all over the atlas, who now in a far country
remembers the first river, the first
field, bricks, and lumber dumped in it ready for building,
that new smell, and remembers
the walls of the garden, the first light.

## The Picnic

It is the picnic with Ruth in the spring.
Ruth was third on my list of seven girls
But the first two were gone (Betty) or else
Had someone (Ellen has accepted Doug).
Indian Gully the last day of school;
Girls make the lunches for the boys too.
I wrote a note to Ruth in algebra class
Day before the test. She smiled, and nodded.
We left the cars and walked through the young corn
The shoots green as paint and the leaves like tongues
Trembling. Beyond the fence where we stood
Some wild strawberry flowered by an elm tree
And Jack-in-the-pulpit was olive ripe.
A blackbird fled as I crossed, and showed
A spot of gold or red under its quick wing.
I held the wire for Ruth and watched the whip
Of her long, striped skirt as she followed.
Three freckles blossomed on her thin, white back
Underneath the loop where the blouse buttoned.
We went for our lunch away from the rest,
Stretched in the new grass, our heads close
Over unknown things wrapped up in wax papers.
Ruth tried for the same, I forget what it was,
And our hands were together. She laughed,
And a breeze caught the edge of her little
Collar and the edge of her brown, loose hair
That touched my cheek. I turned my face in-
to the gentle fall. I saw how sweet it smelled.
She didn't move her head or take her hand.
I felt a soft caving in my stomach

As at the top of the highest slide
When I had been a child, but was not afraid,
And did not know why my eyes moved with wet
As I brushed her cheek with my lips and brushed
Her lips with my own lips. She said to me
Jack, Jack, different than I had ever heard,
Because she wasn't calling me, I think,
Or telling me. She used my name to
Talk in another way I wanted to know.
She laughed again and then she took her hand;
I gave her what we both had touched – can't
Remember what it was, and we ate the lunch.
Afterward we walked in the small, cool creek
Our shoes off, her skirt hitched, and she smiling,
My pants rolled, and then we climbed up the high
Side of Indian Gully and looked
Where we had been, our hands together again.
It was then some bright thing came in my eyes,
Starting at the back of them and flowing
Suddenly through my head and down my arms
And stomach and my bare legs that seemed not
To stop in feet, not to feel the red earth
Of the Gully, as though we hung in a
Touch of birds. There was a word in my throat
With the feeling and I knew the first time
What it meant and I said, it's beautiful.
Yes, she said, and I felt the sound and word
In my hand join the sound and word in hers
As in one name said, or in one cupped hand.
We put back on our shoes and socks and we
Sat in the grass awhile, crosslegged, under
A blowing tree, not saying anything.
And Ruth played with shells she found in the creek,
As I watched. Her small wrist which was so sweet
To me turned by her breast and the shells dropped
Green, white, blue, easily into her lap,

Passing light through themselves. She gave the pale
Shells to me, and got up and touched her hips
With her light hands, and we walked down slowly
To play the school games with the others.


## A Trip to Four or Five Towns
### (To James Wright)

### I

THE gold-coloured skin of my Lebanese friends.
Their deep, lightless eyes.
The serene, inner, careful
balance they share. The conjugal
smile of either for either.

### II

This bellychilling, shoe soaking, factory-
dug-up-hill smothering Pittsburgh weather!
I wait for a cab in the smart mahogany
lobby of the seminary.
The marble *Pietà* is flanked around
with fake fern. She cherishes her dead son
stretched along her womb he triple crossed.
A small, slippered priest
pads up. Whom do you seek, my son?
Father, I've come in out of the rain.
I seek refuge from the elemental tears,
for my heavy, earthen body runs to grief
and I am apt to drown
in this small and underhanded rain
that drops its dross so delicately
on the hairs of the flowers, my father,
and follows down the veins of leaves
weeping quiet in the wood.

My yellow cab never came,
but I did not confess
beneath the painted Jesus Christ. I left
and never saved myself at all
That night in that late, winter rain.


### III

In Washington, was it spring?
I took the plane.
I heard, on either side,
the soft executives, manicured and
fat, fucking this and fucking that.
My heavy second breakfast
lay across my lap.
At port, in the great concourse,
I could not walk to city bus
or cab? or limousine?
I sweat with shock, with havoc
Of the hundred kinds of time,
trembling like a man away from home.

At the National Stripshow
where the girls wriggle right
and slow, I find I want to see in
under the sequin step in.
And in my later dream of the negro girl's room
strong with ancient sweat and with her thick
aroma, I seem to play a melodrama
as her great, red dog barks twice
and I stab it with my pocket knife.


### IV

In Richmond the azalea banks
burst in rose and purple gullies by the car,
muted in the soft, wet

April twilight. The old estates
were pruned and rolled fresh
with spring, with splendour, touch-
ing the graceful stride of the boy who brings the paper.

v

My friend has a red-headed mother
capable of love in any kind
of weather. I am not sure
what she passes to her daughters
but from her brown eye and from her breast
she passes wit and spunk to her big sons.
And she is small and pleased when they put
their arms around her, having caught her.
They cut the grass naked to the waist.
They cure the handsome skins of chipmunks and of snakes.
And when they wake in their attic room
they climb down the ladder, half
asleep, feeling the rungs' pressure
on their bare feet, shirt tails out,
brown eyes shut. They eat
what she cooks. One shot a gorgeous coloured hawk
and posed with it, proud, arms and full wings
spread. And one, at the beach,
balanced on his hands, posed
stripped, in the void of sand,
limbs a rudder in the wind,
amid the lonely, blasted wood.
And two sons run swift roans in the high, summer grass.
Now I would guess
her daughters had at least this same
grace and beauty as their mother,
though I have only seen their picture.
I know she is happy with her three
strong sons about her, for they are not clumsy
(one, calmed, so calmly,

bends a good ear to his guitar)
and they are not dull:
one built a small electric shaft topped with a glowing ball.

## VI

In New York I got drunk, to tell the truth,
and almost got locked up when a beat
friend with me took a leak in a telephone booth.
(E. E. Cummings on the Paris lawn.
'Reprieve pisseur Américain!')
At two o'clock he got knocked out
horning in with the girl in the room over him.
Her boy friend was still sober,
and too thin. I saw the blood of a poet
flow on the sidewalk. Oh, if I mock,
it is without heart. I thought
of the torn limbs of Orpheus
scattered in the grass on the hills of Thrace.
Do poets have to have such trouble with the female race?
I do not know. But if they bleed
I lose heart also.
When he reads, ah, when he reads, small but deep-voiced,
he reads well: now weeps, now is cynical,
his large, horned eyes very black and tearful.

And when we visited a poet father
we rode to Jersey on a motor scooter.
My tie and tweeds looped in the winds
I choked in the wake
of the Holland Pipe, and cops,
under glass like carps, eyed us.
That old father was so mellow and generous –
easy to pain,
white, open and at peace, and of good taste,
like his Rutherford house.
And he read, very loud and regal,
sixteen new poems based on paintings by Breughel!

VII

The last night out,
before I climbed on the formal
Capital Viscount and was shot home
high, pure, and clear,
seemed like the right time
to disappear.

*Early in the Morning*

EARLY in the morning
The dark Queen said,
'The trumpets are warning
There's trouble ahead.'
Spent with carousing,
With wine-soaked wits,
Antony drowsing
Whispered, 'It's
Too cold a morning
To get out of bed.'

The army's retreating,
The fleet has fled,
Caesar is beating
His drums through the dead.
'Antony, horses!
We'll get away,
Gather our forces
For another day . . .'
'It's a cold morning,'
Antony said.

Caesar Augustus
Cleared his phlegm.
'Corpses digust us.
Cover them.'
Caesar Augustus
In his time lay
Dying, and just as
Cold as they,
On the cold morning
Of a cold day.

## The Ash and the Oak

WHEN men discovered freedom first
The fighting was on foot,
They were encouraged by their thirst
And promises of loot,
And when it feathered and bows boomed
Their virtue was a root.

O the ash and the oak and the willow tree
And green grows the grass on the infantry!

At Malplaquet and Waterloo
They were polite and proud,
They primed their guns with billets-doux
And, as they fired, bowed.
At Appomattox too, it seems
Some things were understood.

O the ash and the oak and the willow tree
And green grows the grass on the infantry!

But at Verdun and at Bastogne
There was a great recoil,
The blood was bitter to the bone
The trigger to the soul,
And death was nothing if not dull,
A hero was a fool.

O the ash and the oak and the willow tree
And that's an end of the infantry!

## To the Western World

A SIREN sang, and Europe turned away
From the high castle and the shepherd's crook.
Three caravels went sailing to Cathay
On the strange ocean, and the captains shook
Their banners out across the Mexique Bay.

And in our early days we did the same.
Remembering our fathers in their wreck
We crossed the sea from Palos where they came
And saw, enormous to the little deck,
A shore in silence waiting for a name.

The treasures of Cathay were never found.
In this America, this wilderness
Where the axe echoes with a lonely sound,
The generations labour to possess
And grave by grave we civilize the ground.


## The Riders Held Back

ONE morning, as we travelled in the fields
        Of air and dew
With trumpets, and above the painted shields
        The banners flew,

We came upon three ladies, wreathed in roses,
        Where, hand in hand,
They danced – three slender, gentle, naked ladies,
        All in a woodland.

They'd been to the best schools in Italy;
        Their legs were Greek,
Their collarbones, as fine as jewellery,
        Their eyes, antique.

'Why do lambs skip and shepherds shout "Ut hoy!"?
　　　　Why do you dance?'
Said one, 'It is an intellectual joy,
　　　　The Renaissance.

'As do the stars in heaven, ruled by Three,
　　　　We twine and move.
It is the music of Astronomy,
　　　　Not men, we love.

'And as we dance, the beasts and flowers do;
　　　　The fields of wheat
Sway like our arms; the curving hills continue
　　　　The curves of our feet.

'Here Raphael comes to paint; the thrushes flute
　　　　To Petrarch's pen.
But Michael is not here, who carved the brute
　　　　Unfinished men.'

They danced again, and on the mountain heights
　　　　There seemed to rise
Towers and ramparts glittering with lights,
　　　　Like Paradise.

How the bright morning passed, I cannot say.
　　　　We woke and found
The dancers gone; and heard, far, far away,
　　　　The trumpet sound.

We galloped to it. In the forest then
　　　　Banners and shields
Were strewn like leaves; and there were many slain
　　　　In the dark fields.

LOUIS SIMPSON

## Walt Whitman at Bear Mountain

*'... life which does not give the preference to any other life, of any previous period, which therefore prefers its own existence ...'*

ORTEGA Y GASSET

NEITHER on horseback nor seated,
But like himself, squarely on two feet,
The poet of death and lilacs
Loafs by the footpath. Even the bronze looks alive
Where it is folded like cloth. And he seems friendly.

'Where is the Mississippi panorama
And the girl who played the piano?
Where are you, Walt?
The Open Road goes to the used-car lot.

'Where is the nation you promised?
These houses built of wood sustain
Colossal snows,
And the light above the street is sick to death.

'As for the people – see how they neglect you!
Only a poet pauses to read the inscription.'

'I am here,' he answered.
'It seems you have found me out.
Yet, did I not warn you that it was Myself
I advertised? Were my words not sufficiently plain?

'I gave no prescriptions,
And those who have taken my moods for prophecies
Mistake the matter.'
Then, vastly amused – 'Why do you reproach me?
I freely confess I am wholly disreputable.
Yet I am happy, because you have found me out.'

A crocodile in wrinkled metal loafing ...

Then all the realtors,
Pickpockets, salesmen, and the actors performing

Official scenarios,
Turned a deaf ear, for they had contracted
American dreams.

But the man who keeps a store on a lonely road,
And the housewife who knows she's dumb,
And the earth, are relieved.

All that grave weight of America
Cancelled! Like Greece and Rome.
The future in ruins!
The castles, the prisons, the cathedrals
Unbuilding, and roses
Blossoming from the stones that are not there . . .

The clouds are lifting from the high Sierras,
The Bay mists clearing;
And the angel in the gate, the flowering plum,
Dances like Italy, imagining red.

## There Is

### I

LOOK! From my window there's a view
of city streets
where only lives as dry as tortoises
can crawl – the Gallapagos of desire.

There is the day of Negroes with red hair
and the day of insane women on the subway;
there is the day of the word Trieste
and the night of the blind man with the electric guitar.

But I have no profession. Like a spy
I read the papers – Situations Wanted.
Surely there is a secret
which, if I knew it, would change everything!

## II

I have the poor man's nerve-tic, irony.
I see through the illusions of the age!
The bells tolls, and the hearse advances,
and the mourners follow, for my entertainment.

I tread the burning pavement,
the streets where drunkards stretch
like photographs of civil death
and trumpets strangle in electric shelves.

The mannequins stare at me scornfully.
I know they are pretending
all day to be in earnest.
And can it be that love is an illusion?

When darkness falls on the enormous street
the air is filled with Eros, whispering.
Eyes, mouths, contrive to meet
in silence, fearing they may be prevented.

## III

O businessmen like ruins,
bankers who are Bastilles,
widows, sadder than the shores of lakes,
then you were happy, when you still could tremble!

But all night long my window
sheds tears of light.
I seek the word. The word is not forthcoming.
O syllables of light . . . O dark cathedral . . .

## My Father in the Night Commanding No

MY father in the night commanding No
Has work to do. Smoke issues from his lips;
    He reads in silence.
The frogs are croaking and the streetlamps glow.

And then my mother winds the gramophone;
The Bride of Lammermoor begins to shriek –
    Or reads a story
About a prince, a castle, and a dragon.

The moon is glittering above the hill.
I stand before the gateposts of the King –
    So runs the story –
Of Thule, at midnight when the mice are still.

And I have been in Thule! It has come true –
The journey and the danger of the world,
    All that there is
To bear and to enjoy, endure and do.

Landscapes, seascapes . . . where have I been led?
The names of cities – Paris, Venice, Rome –
    Held out their arms.
A feathered god, seductive, went ahead.

Here is my house. Under a red rose tree
A child is swinging; another gravely plays.
    They are not surprised
That I am here; they were expecting me.

And yet my father sits and reads in silence,
My mother sheds a tear, the moon is still,
    And the dark wind
Is murmuring that nothing ever happens.

Beyond his jurisdiction as I move
Do I not prove him wrong? And yet, it's true
  *They* will not change
There, on the stage of terror and of love.

The actors in that playhouse always sit
In fixed positions – father, mother, child
  With painted eyes.
How sad it is to be a little puppet!

Their heads are wooden. And you once pretended
To understand them! Shake them as you will,
  They cannot speak.
Do what you will, the comedy is ended.

Father, why did you work? Why did you weep,
Mother? Was the story so important?
  '*Listen!*' the wind
Said to the children, and they fell asleep.

## The Mountain Cemetery

WITH their harsh leaves old rhododendrons fill
The crevices in grave plots' broken stones.
The bees renew the blossoms they destroy,
While in the burning air the pines rise still,
Commemorating long forgotten biers,
Whose roots replace the semblance of these bones.

The weight of cool, of imperceptible dust
That came from nothing and to nothing came
Is light within the earth and on the air.
The change that so renews itself is just.
The enormous, sundry platitude of death
Is for these bones, bees, trees, and leaves the same.

And splayed upon the ground and through the trees
The mountains' shadow fills and cools the air,
Smoothing the shape of headstones to the earth.
The rhododendrons suffer with the bees
Whose struggles loose ripe petals to the earth,
The heaviest burden it shall ever bear.

Our hard earned knowledge fits us for such sleep.
Although the spring must come, it passes too
To form the burden suffered for what comes.
Whatever we would give our souls to keep
Is only part of what we call the soul;
What we of time would threaten to undo

All time in its slow scrutiny has done.
For on the grass that starts about the feet
The body's shadow turns, to shape in time,
Soon grown preponderant with creeping shade,
The final shadow that is turn of earth;
And what seems won paid for as in defeat.

## The Prince

*. . . si quid mea carmina possunt, nulla dies umquam memori vos eximet aevo, dum domus Aeneae Capitoli immobile saxum accolet . . .*

I COME to tell you that my son is dead.
Americans have shot him as a spy.
Our heritage has wasted what it shaped,
And he the ruin's proof. I suffered once
My self-destruction like a pleasure, gave
Over to what I could not understand
The one whom all my purpose was to save.
Deceit was the desire to be deceived,
For, when I kissed illusion's face, tears gushed
Warm under anguished eye-lids, and were dried
By new desire that chilled me like a wind —
As if it were defeat being alive
And hurt should yet restore me and be joy,
Joy without cause! Longing without an end,
That could not love the thing which it desired.
Through all that time I craved magnificence
Of the doomed fox — black paws, white throat, and red
Coat dragged among crisp yellow leaves, along
A stream trout break all night with glistening rise,
Austere, old lonely grandeur's complete pride
The pack's mute victim, while the crimson eyes
Glitter with Epicurus's innocence.
Giddy with lack of hope, my mind foresaw
Itself, still barely human and by duress
Bound in heroic trance, take glittering
Impassive armour up and crowd the niche
Of time with iron necessity; and hard
With loss and disbelief approved its choice.

This is the time's presumption: ignorance
Denies what we have been and might become.
So will and thought are mirrors of themselves.

Uniquely the strange object I might know,
I chose to live, who else had found no reason
In vanity's contempt, by simple faith
In what had been before me, and restored
The name of duty to a shadow, spent
Of meaning and obscure with rage and doubt
Intense as cold. My son, who was the heir
To every hope and trust, grew out of caring
Into the form of loss as I had done,
And then betrayed me who betrayed him first.
You know despair's authority, the rite
And exaltation by which we are governed,
A state absurd with wrath that we are human,
Nothing, to which our nature would submit.
Such was the German state. Yet, like a fool,
I hated it, my image, and was glad
When he refused its service; now I know
That even his imprisonment was mine,
A gesture by the will to break the will.
Honouring it, I dreamed again the fierce
Abandonment to what one hates, the fox
Joyful in pain and helplessness. O sages,
Of whom we are the merest shades, you are
The undemanding whom indifference
Has least defiled, those few whose innocence
Is earned by long distraction with minute
And slow corruption proving all they know,
Till patience, young in what may come to pass,
Is reconciled to what its love permits,
And is not proud that knowledge must be so.

*

By what persuasion he saw fit to change
Allegiance, none need wonder. Let there be,
However, no mistake: those who deny
What they believe is true, desire shall mock
And crime's uncertain promise shall deceive

Alas, that he was not a German soldier
In his apostasy, but would put on
The parody of what caprice put off.
Enemy in disguise, the uniform
And speech of what the sceptic heart requires –
Ruthless the irony that is its thought!
The soldier's death should find him unaware,
The breathless air close round him as sleep falls,
Sudden with ripeness, heavy with release.
Thereby the guileless tranquilly are strong:
The man is overwhelmed, the deed remains.
Flesh of my flesh, bewildered to despair
And fallen outside the limits of my name,
Forever lies apart and meaningless.
I who remain perceive the dear, familiar
Unblemished face of possibility
Drenched by a waste profound with accident,
His childhood face concealed behind my face.
Where is the guile enough to comfort me?

## The Centaur Overheard

ONCE I lived with my brothers, images
Of what we know best and can best become.
What I might be I learned to tell in eyes
Which loved me. Voices formed my name,

Taught me its sound, released me from its dread.
Now they are all gone. When I move, the sound
From dark caves where my hooves disturb the dead
Orders no other purpose. Underground,

Streams urge their ceaseless motion into air.
I stand by springs and drink. Their brimming poise
Repeats the selfish hope of who comes there.
But I do not look, move, or make a noise.

## Adam's Song to Heaven

*'You will be as God, knowing good and evil'*

O DEPTH sufficient to desire,
Ghostly abyss wherein perfection hides,
    Purest effect and cause, you are
The mirror and the image love provides.

    All else is waste, though you reveal
Lightly upon your luminous bent shore
    Colour, shape, odour, weight, and voice,
Bright mocking hints that were not there before.

    And all your progeny time holds
In timeless birth and death. But, when, for bliss,
    Loneliness would possess its like,
Mine is the visage yours leans down to kiss.

    Beautiful you are, fair deceit!
Knowledge is joy where your unseeing eyes
    Shine with the tears that I have wept
To be the sum of all your thoughts devise.

    Flawless you are, unlimited
By other than yourself, yet suffer pain
    Of the nostalgias I have felt
For love beyond the end your eyes contain;

    Then, solitary, drift, inert,
Through the abyss where you would have me go,
    And, lost to your desire, at last
Ravish the waste for what you cannot know.

    What are you then! Delirium
Receives the image I despair to keep,
    And knowledge in your sombre depth
Embraces your perfection and your sleep.

## Le Rêve

I DREAMED last night I dreamed, and in that sleep
You called me from the stair, as if the dead
Command all fragile sleepers to awake
And free them from their darkened wandering.
I knew that you would come into the room.
I waited for the sudden tug and slant
Upon the edge of my vague spectral bed,
The mattress tilted down, the springs gone tense.
I woke, looked at my watch, and sucked my breath.
There in my stead, still waiting, and still true,
Lay him who dreamed me still and, maybe, you.

*Beyond the Hunting Woods*

I SPEAK of that great house
Beyond the hunting woods,
Turreted and towered
In nineteenth-century style,
Where fireflies by the hundreds
Leap in the long grass,
Odour of jessamine
And roses, canker-bit,
Recalling famous times
When dame and maiden sipped
Sassafras or wild
Elderberry wine,
While far in the hunting woods
Men after their red hounds
Pursued the mythic beast.

I ask it of a stranger,
In all that great house finding
Not any living thing,
Or of the wind and the weather,
What charm was in that wine
That they should vanish so,
Ladies in their stiff
Bone and clean of limb,
And over the hunting woods
What mist had maddened them
That gentlemen should lose
Not only the beast in view
But Belle and Ginger too,
Nor home from the hunting woods
Ever, ever come?

## On the Death of Friends in Childhood

WE shall not ever meet them bearded in heaven,
Nor sunning themselves among the bald of hell;
If anywhere, in the deserted schoolyard at twilight,
Forming a ring, perhaps, or joining hands
In games whose very names we have forgotten.
Come, memory, let us seek them there in the shadows.

## Here in Katmandu

WE have climbed the mountain
There's nothing more to do.
It is terrible to come down
To the valley
Where, amidst many flowers,
One thinks of snow,

As, formerly, amidst snow,
Climbing the mountain,
One thought of flowers,
Tremulous, ruddy with dew,
In the valley.
One caught their scent coming down.

It is difficult to adjust, once down,
To the absence of snow.
Clear days, from the valley,
One looks up at the mountain.
What else is there to do?
Prayerwheels, flowers!

Let the flowers
Fade, the prayerwheels run down.
What have these to do

With us who have stood atop the snow
Atop the mountain,
Flags seen from the valley?

It might be possible to live in the valley,
To bury oneself among flowers,
If one could forget the mountain,
How, setting out before dawn,
Blinded with snow,
One knew what to do.

Meanwhile it is not easy here in Katmandu,
Especially when to the valley
That wind which means snow
Elsewhere, but here means flowers,
Comes down,
As soon it must, from the mountain.


## Another Song

MERRY the green, the green hill shall be merry.
Hungry, the owlet shall seek out the mouse,
And Jack his Joan, but they shall never marry.

And snows shall fly, the big flakes fat and furry.
Lonely, the traveller shall seek out the house,
And Jack his Joan, but they shall never marry.

Weary the soldiers go, and come back weary,
Up a green hill and down the withered hill,
And Jack from Joan, and they shall never marry.

## Counting the Mad

THIS one was put in a jacket,
This one was sent home,
This one was given bread and meat
But would eat none,
And this one cried No No No No
All day long.

This one looked at the window
As though it were a wall,
This one saw things that were not there,
This one things that were,
And this one cried No No No No
All day long.

This one thought himself a bird,
This one a dog,
And this one thought himself a man,
An ordinary man,
And cried and cried No No No No
All day long.

## On a Painting by Patient B of the Independence State Hospital for the Insane

I

THESE seven houses have learned to face one another,
But not at the expected angles. Those silly brown lumps,
That are probably meant for hills and not other houses,
After ages of being themselves, though naturally slow,
Are learning to be exclusive without offending.
The arches and entrances (down to the right out of sight)
Have mastered the lesson of remaining closed.
And even the skies keep a certain understandable distance,
For these are the houses of the very rich.

## II

One sees their children playing with leopards, tamed
At great cost, or perhaps it is only other children,
For none of these objects is anything more than a spot,
And perhaps there are not any children but only leopards
Playing with leopards, and perhaps there are only the spots.
And the little maids from the windows hanging like tongues,
Calling the children in, admiring the leopards,
Are the dashes a child might represent motion by means of,
Or dazzlement possibly, the brilliance of solid-gold houses.

## III

The clouds resemble those empty balloons in cartoons
Which approximate silence. These clouds, if clouds they are
(And not the smoke from the seven aspiring chimneys),
The more one studies them the more it appears
They too have expressions. One might almost say
They have their habits, their wrong opinions, that their
Impassivity masks an essentially lovable foolishness,
And they will be given names by those who live under them
Not public like mountains' but private like companions'.

### Where We Must Look for Help

THE dove returns; it found no resting place;
It was in flight all night above the shaken seas;
Beneath ark eaves
The dove shall magnify the tiger's bed;
Give the dove peace.
The split-tail swallows leave the sill at dawn;
At dusk, blue swallows shall return.
On the third day the crow shall fly;
The crow, the crow, the spider-coloured crow,
The crow shall find new mud to walk upon.

### Sunday in Glastonbury

IT is out in the flimsy suburbs,
Where the light seems to shine through the walls.

My black shoes stand on the floor
Like two open graves.

The curtains do not know what to hope for,
But they are obedient.

How strange to think of India!
Wealth is nothing but lack of people.

ROBERT BLY

## Awakening

WE are approaching sleep: the chestnut blossoms in the
mind
Mingle with thoughts of pain
And the long roots of barley, bitterness
As of the oak roots staining the waters dark
In Louisiana, the wet streets soaked with rain
And sodden blossoms, out of this
We have come, a tunnel softly hurtling into darkness.

The storm is coming. The small farmhouse in Minnesota
Is hardly strong enough for the storm.
Darkness, darkness in grass, darkness in trees.
Even the water in wells trembles.
Bodies give off darkness, and chrysanthemums
Are dark, and horses, who are bearing great loads of hay
To the deep barns where the dark air is moving from corners.

Lincoln's statue and the traffic. From the long past
Into the long present
A bird, forgotten in these pressures, warbling,
As the great wheel turns around, grinding
The living in water.
Washing, continual washing, in water now stained
With blossoms and rotting logs,
Cries, half-muffled, from beneath the earth, the living
awakened at last like the dead.

## Poem Against the British

### I

THE wind through the box-elder trees
Is like rides at dusk on a white horse,
Wars for your country, and fighting the British.

### II

I wonder if Washington listened to the trees.
All morning I have been sitting in grass,
Higher than my eyes, beneath trees,
And listening upward, to the wind in leaves.
Suddenly I realize there is one thing more:
There is also the wind through the high grass.

### III

There are palaces, boats, silence among white buildings,
Iced drinks on marble tops among cool rooms;
It is also good to be poor, and listen to the wind.

## Driving toward the Lac Qui Parle River

### I

I AM driving; it is dusk; Minnesota.
The stubble field catches the last growth of sun.
The soybeans are breathing on all sides.
Old men are sitting before their houses on carseats
In the small towns. I am happy,
The moon rising above the turkey sheds.

### II

The small world of the car
Plunges through the deep fields of the night,
On the road from Willmar to Milan.

This solitude covered with iron
Moves through the fields of night
Penetrated by the noise of crickets.

### III

Nearly to Milan, suddenly a small bridge,
And water kneeling in the moonlight.
In small towns the houses are built right on the ground;
The lamplight falls on all fours in the grass.
When I reach the river, the full moon covers it;
A few people are talking low in a boat.

## Hunting Pheasants in a Cornfield

### I

WHAT is so strange about a tree alone in an open field?
It is a willow tree. I walk around and around it.
The body is strangely torn, and cannot leave it.
At last I sit down beneath it.

### II

It is a willow tree alone in acres of dry corn.
Its leaves are scattered around its trunk, and around me,
Brown now, and speckled with delicate black.
Only the cornstalks now can make a noise.

### III

The sun is cold, burning through the frosty distances of space.
The weeds are frozen to death long ago.
Why then do I love to watch
The sun moving on the chill skin of the branches?

IV

The mind has shed leaves alone for years.
It stands apart with small creatures near its roots.
I am happy in this ancient place,
A spot easily caught sight of above the corn,
If I were a young animal ready to turn home at dusk.


## A Busy Man Speaks

NOT to the mother of solitude will I give myself
Away, not to the mother of art, nor the mother
Of the ocean, nor the mother of the snake and the fire;
Not to the mother of love,
Nor the mother of conversation, nor the mother
Of the downcast face, nor the mother of the solitude of
    death;
Not to the mother of the night full of crickets,
Nor the mother of the open fields, nor the mother of Christ.

But I will give myself to the father of righteousness, the
    father
Of cheerfulness, who is also the father of rocks,
Who is also the father of perfect gestures;
From the Chase National Bank
An arm of flame has come, and I am drawn
To the desert, to the parched places, to the landscape of
    zeros;
And I shall give myself away to the father of righteousness,
The stones of cheerfulness, the steel of money, the father of
    rocks.

## Poem in Three Parts

### I

Oh, on an early morning I think I shall live forever?
I am wrapped in my joyful flesh,
As the grass is wrapped in its clouds of green.

### II

Rising from a bed, where I dreamt
Of long rides past castles and hot coals,
The sun lies happily on my knees;
I have suffered and survived the night,
Bathed in dark water, like any blade of grass.

### III

The strong leaves of the box-elder tree,
Plunging in the wind, call us to disappear
Into the wilds of the universe,
Where we shall sit at the foot of a plant,
And live forever, like the dust.

## The Possibility of New Poetry

Singing of Niagara, and the Huron squaws,
The chaise-longue, the periwinkles in a rage like snow,
Dillinger like a dark wind.
Intelligence, cover the advertising men with clear water,
And the factories with merciless space,
So that the strong-haunched woman
By the blazing stove of the sun, the moon,
May come home to me, sitting on the naked wood
In another world, and all the Shell stations
Folded in a faint light.

## After the Industrial Revolution,
## All Things Happen at Once

Now we enter a strange world, where the Hessian Christmas
Still goes on, and Washington has not reached the other
  shore;
The Whiskey Boys
Are gathering again on the meadows of Pennsylvania
And the Republic is still sailing on the open sea

In 1956 I saw a black angel in Washington, dancing
On a barge, saying, 'Let us now divide kennel dogs
And hunting dogs'; Henry Cabot Lodge, in New York,
Talking of sugar cane in Cuba; Ford,
In Detroit, drinking mother's milk;
Henry Cabot Lodge, saying, 'Remember the Maine!'
Ford, saying, 'History is bunk!'
And Wilson, saying, 'What is good for General Motors –'

Who is it, singing? Don't you hear singing?
It is the dead of Cripple Creek;
Coxey's army
Like turkeys are singing from the tops of trees!
And the Whiskey Boys are drunk outside Philadelphia.

## Sleet Storm on the Merritt Parkway

I look out at the white sleet covering the still streets,
As we drive through Scarsdale –
The sleet began falling as we left Connecticut,
And the wet winter leaves swirled in the wet air after cars
Like hands suddenly turned over in a conversation.
Now the frost has nearly buried the short green grass of
  March;

Seeing the sheets of sleet untouched on the wide streets,
I think of the many comfortable homes stretching for miles,
Two and three storeys, solid, with polished floors,
With white curtains in the upstairs bedrooms,
And small perfume flagons of black glass on the window sills,
And warm bathrooms with guest towels, and electric lights –
What a magnificent place for a child to grow up!
And yet the children end in the river of price-fixing,
Or in the snowy field of the insane asylum.
The sleet falls – so many cars moving toward New York –
Last night we argued about the Marines invading Guatemala
      in 1947,
The United Fruit Company had one water spigot for 200
      families,
And the ideals of America, our freedom to criticize,
The slave systems of Rome and Greece, and no one agreed.


## Andrew Jackson's Speech

*Dido to Aeneas: 'I have broke faith with the ashes of Sichaeus.'*

I HEARD Andrew Jackson say, as he closed his Virgil:

'The harsh ravishers in Detroit, inheritors of the soot
   Of chimney boys, when they raised the mighty poor,
   Broke faith with the cinders of Sichaeus.

'I shot to save the honour of my wife;
   And I would shoot again, to save my people.
   The Republic lies in the blossoms of Washington.

'The poor have been raised up by the Revolution.
   Washington, riding in cold snow at Valley Forge,
   Warned the poor never to take another husband.'

His voice rose in the noisy streets of Detroit.

---

### After Lorca
#### (For M. Marti)

THE church is a business, and the rich
are the business men.
                        When they pull on the bells, the
poor come piling in and when a poor man dies, he has a
    wooden
cross, and they rush through the ceremony.

But when a rich man dies, they
drag out the Sacrament
and a golden Cross, and go *doucement, doucement*
to the cemetery.

And the poor love it
and think it's crazy.

### I Know a Man

As I sd to my
friend, because I am
always talking, – John, I

sd, which was not his
name, the darkness sur-
rounds us, what

can we do against
it, or else, shall we &
why not, buy a goddamn big car,

drive, he sd, for
christ's sake, look
out where yr going.


## The Hill

IT is sometime since I have been
to what it was had once turned me backwards,
and made my head into
a cruel instrument.

It is simple
to confess. Then done,
to walk away, walk away,
to come again.

But that form, I must answer,
is dead in me, completely,
and I will not allow it
to reappear —

Saith perversity, the wilful,
the magnanimous cruelty,
which is in me
like a hill.


## The Signboard

THE quieter the people are
the slower the time passes

until there is a solitary man
sitting in the figure of silence.

Then scream at him,
come here you idiot it's going to go off.

A face that is no face
but the features, of a face, pasted

on a face until that face
is faceless, answers by

a being nothing there
where there was a man.


## The Cracks

DON'T step
so lightly. Break
your back, missed
the step. Don't go

away mad, lady in
the nightmare. You
are central,
even necessary.

I will attempt to describe you.
I will be completely without
face, a lost
chance, nothing at all left.

'Well,' he said
as he was leaving,
'blood
tells.'

But you remembered quickly
other times, other faces,
and I slipped between the good
intentions, breathlessly.

What a good boy am I who
wants to. Will you,
mother, come quickly,
won't you. Why not

go quietly, be left
with a memory
or an insinuation or two
of cracks in a pavement.


### For Love

*(For Bobbie)*

YESTERDAY I wanted to
speak of it, that sense above
the others to me
important because all

that I know derives
from what it teaches me.
Today, what is it that
is finally so helpless,

different, despairs of its own
statement, wants to
turn away, endlessly
to turn away.

If the moon did not . . .
no, if you did not
I wouldn't either, but
what would I not

do, what prevention, what
thing so quickly stopped.
That is love yesterday
or tomorrow, not

now. Can I eat
what you give me. I
have not earned it. Must
I think of everything

as earned. Now love also
becomes a reward so
remote from me I have
only made it with my mind.

Here is tedium,
despair, a painful
sense of isolation and
whimsical if pompous

self-regard. But that image
is only of the mind's
vague structure, vague to me
because it is my own.

Love, what do I think
to say. I cannot say it.
What have you become to ask,
what have I made you into,

companion, good company,
crossed legs with skirt, or
soft body under
the bones of the bed.

Nothing says anything
but that which it wishes
would come true, fears
what else might happen in

some other place, some
other time not this one.
A voice in my place, an
echo of that only in yours.

Let me stumble into
not the confession but
the obsession I begin with
now. For you

also (also)
some time beyond place, or
place beyond time, no
mind left to

say anything at all,
that face gone, now.
Into the company of love
it all returns.

## Kore

As I was walking
  I came upon
chance walking
  the same road upon.

As I sat down
  by chance to move
later
  if and as I might,

light the wood was,
  light and green,
and what I saw
  before I had not seen.

It was a lady
  accompanied
by goat men
  leading her.

Her hair held earth.
        Her eyes were dark.
A double flute
        made her move.

'O love,
        where are you
leading
        me now?'

## The Rain

ALL night the sound had
come back again,
and again falls
this quiet, persistent rain.

What am I to myself
that must be remembered,
insisted upon,
so often? Is it

that never the ease,
even the hardness,
of rain falling
will have for me

something other than this,
something not so insistent –
am I to be locked in this
final uneasiness.

Love, if you love me,
lie next to me.
Be for me, like rain,
the getting out

of the tiredness, the fatuousness, the semi-
lust of intentional indifference.
Be wet
with a decent happiness.

---

## *The Power Station*

THINK back now to that cleft
In the live rock. A deep voice filled the cave,
Raving up out of cells each time in some way left
Huger and vaguer. There was a kind of nave

Strewn with potsherd and bone,
The tribe's offspring, converted now, rejoice
In our sane god. But, two or three hours south, not known
To them, the charges of the other's voice

Break into light and churn
Through evening fields. Soon a first town is lit,
Is lived in. Grounded. Green. A truth fit to unlearn
The blind delirium that still utters it.

## *Angel*

ABOVE my desk, whirring and self-important
(Though not much larger than a hummingbird)
In finely woven robes, school of Van Eyck,
Hovers an evidently angelic visitor.
He points one index finger out the window
At winter snatching to its heart,
To crystal vacancy, the misty
Exhalations of houses and of people running home
From the cold sun pounding on the sea;
While with the other hand
He indicates the piano
Where the Sarabande No. 1 lies open
At a passage I shall never master

But which has already, and effortlessly mastered me.
He drops his jaw as if to say, or sing,
Between the world God made
And this music of Satie,
Each glimpsed through veils, but whole,
Radiant and willed,
Demanding praise, demanding surrender,
How can you sit there with your notebook?
What do you think you are doing?'
However he says nothing – wisely: I could mention
Flaws in God's world, or Satie's; and for that matter
How did he come by *his* taste for Satie?
Half to tease him, I turn back to my page,
Its phrases thus far clotted, unconnected.
The tiny angel shakes his head.
There is no smile on his round, hairless face.
He does not want even these few lines written.


## Childlessness

THE weather of this winter night, my mistress
Ranting and raining, wakes me. Her cloak blown back
To show the lining's dull lead foil
Sweeps along asphalt. Houses
Look blindly on; one glimmers through a blind.
Outside, I hear her tricklings
Arraign my little plot:
Had it or not agreed
To transplantation for the common good
Of certain rare growths yielding guaranteed
Gold pollen, gender of suns, large, hardy,
Enviable blooms? But in my garden
Nothing is planted. Neither
Is that glimmering window mine.

I lie and think about the rain,
How it has been drawn up from the impure ocean,
From gardens lightly, deliberately tainted;
How it falls back, time after time,
Through poisons visible at sunset
When the enchantress, masked as friend, unfurls
Entire bolts of voluminous pistachio,
Saffron, and rose.
These, as I fall back to sleep,
And other slow colours clothe me, glide
To rest, then burst along my limbs like buds,
Like bombs from the navigator's vantage,
Waking me, lulling me. Later I am shown
The erased metropolis reassembled
On sampans, freighted each
With toddlers, holy dolls, dead ancestors.
One tiny monkey puzzles over fruit.
The vision rises and falls, the garland
Gently takes root
In the sea's coma. Hours go by
Before I can stand to own
A sky stained red, a world
Clad only in rags, threadbare,
Dabbling the highway's ice with blood.
A world. The cloak thrown down for it to wear
In token of past servitude
Has fallen onto the shoulders of my parents
Whom it is eating to the bone.

## After Greece

LIGHT into the olive entered
And was oil. Rain made the huge pale stones
Shine from within. The moon turned his hair white
Who next stepped from between the columns,
Shielding his eyes. All through
The countryside were old ideas
Found lying open to the elements.
Of the gods' houses only
A minor premise here and there
Would be balancing the heaven of fixed stars
Upon a Doric capital. The rest
Lay spilled, their fluted drums half sunk in cyclamen
Or deep in water's biting clarity
Which just barely upheld me
The next week, when I sailed for home.
But where is home – these walls?
These limbs? The very spaniel underfoot
Races in sleep, toward what?
It is autumn. I did not invite
Those guests, windy and brittle, who drink my liquor.
Returning from a walk I find
The bottles filled with spleen, my room itself
Smeared by reflection on to the far hemlocks.
I some days flee in dream
Back to the exposed porch of the maidens
Only to find my great-great-grandmothers
Erect there, peering
Into a globe of red Bohemian glass.
As it swells and sinks, I call up
Graces, Furies, Fates, removed
To my country's warm, lit halls, with rivets forced
Through draper, and nothing left to bear.
They seem anxious to know
What holds up heaven nowadays.

I start explaining how in that vast fire
Were other irons – well, Art, Public Spirit,
Ignorance, Economics, Love of Self,
Hatred of Self, a hundred more,
Each burning to be felt, each dedicated
To sparing us the worst; how I distrust them
As I should have done those ladies; how I want
Essentials: salt, wine, olive, the light, the scream –
No! I have scarcely named you,
And look, in a flash you stand full-grown before me,
Row upon row, Essentials,
Dressed like your sister caryatids
Or tombstone angels jealous of their dead,
With undulant coiffures, lips weathered, cracked by grime,
And faultless eyes gone blank beneath the immense
Zinc and gunmetal northern sky. . . .
Stay then. Perhaps the system
Calls for spirits. This first glass I down
To the last time
I ate and drank in that old world. May I
Also survive its meanings, and my own.

## From *Heart's Needle*

### I

CHILD of my winter, born
When the new fallen soldiers froze
In Asia's steep ravines and fouled the snows,
When I was torn

By love I could not still,
By fear that silenced my cramped mind
To that cold war where, lost, I could not find
My peace in my will,

All those days we could keep
Your mind a landscape of new snow
Where the chilled tenant-farmer finds, below,
His fields asleep

In their smooth covering, white
As quilts to warm the resting bed
Of birth or pain, spotless as paper spread
For me to write,

And thinks: Here lies my land
Unmarked by agony, the lean foot
Of the weasel tracking, the thick trapper's boot;
And I have planned

My chances to restrain
The torments of demented summer or
Increase the deepening harvest here before
It snows again.

IV

No one can tell you why
the season will not wait;
the night I told you I
must leave, you wept a fearful rate
to stay up late.

Now that it's turning Fall,
we go to take our walk
among municipal
flowers, to steal one off its stalk,
to try and talk.

We huff like windy giants
scattering with our breath
gray-headed dandelions;
Spring is the cold wind's aftermath.
The poet saith.

But the asters, too, are gray,
ghost-gray. Last night's cold
is sending on their way
petunias and dwarf marigold,
hunched sick and old.

Like nerves caught in a graph,
the morning-glory vines
frost has erased by half
still scrawl across their rigid twines.
Like broken lines

of verses I can't make.
In its unravelling loom
we find a flower to take,
with some late buds that might still bloom,
back to your room.

Night comes and the stiff dew.
I'm told a friend's child cried
    because a cricket, who
had minstrelled every night outside
        her window, died.

VI

    Easter has come around
again; the river is rising
    over the thawed ground
and the banksides. When you come you bring
    an egg dyed lavender.
We shout along our bank to hear
our voices returning from the hills to meet us.
    We need the landscape to repeat us.

    You lived on this bank first.
While nine months filled your term, we knew
    how your lungs, immersed
in the womb, miraculously grew
    their useless folds till
the fierce, cold air rushed in to fill
them out like bushes thick with leaves. You took your hour,
    caught breath, and cried with your full lung power.

    Over the stagnant bight
we see the hungry bank swallow
    flaunting his free flight
still; we sink in mud to follow
    the killdeer from the grass
that hides her nest. That March there was
rain; the rivers rose; you could hear killdeers flying
    all night over the mudflats crying.

    You bring back how the red-
winged blackbird shrieked, slapping frail wings,
    diving at my head —
I saw where her tough nest, cradled, swings

in tall reeds that must sway
    with the winds blowing every way.
If you recall much, you recall this place. You still
    live nearby – on the opposite hill.


    After the sharp windstorm
    of July Fourth, all that summer
        through the gentle, warm
    afternoons, we heard great chain saws chirr
        like iron locusts. Crews
    of roughneck boys swarmed to cut loose
branches wrenched in the shattering wind, to hack free
    all the torn limbs that could sap the tree.


    In the debris lay
    starlings, dead. Near the park's birdrun
        we surprised one day
    a proud, tan-spatted, buff-brown pigeon.
        In my hands she flapped so
    fearfully that I let her go.
Her keeper came. And we helped snarl her in a net.
    You bring things I'd as soon forget.


    You raise into my head
    a Fall night that I came once more
        to sit on your bed;
    sweat beads stood out on your arms and fore-
        head and you wheezed for breath,
    for help, like some child caught beneath
its comfortable woolly blankets, drowning there.
    Your lungs caught and would not take the air.


    Of all things, only we
    have power to choose that we should die;
        nothing else is free
    in this world to refuse it. Yet I,

who say this, could not raise
myself from bed how many days
to the thieving world. Child, I have another wife,
another child. We try to choose our life.


## The Examination

UNDER the thick beams of that swirly smoking light,
  The black robes are clustering, huddled in together.
Hunching their shoulders, they spread short, broad sleeves
    like night-
  Black grackles' wings and reach out bone-yellow leather-

y fingers, each to each. They are prepared. Each turns
  His single eye – or since one can't discern their eyes,
That reflective, single, moon-pale disc which burns
  Over each brow – to watch this uncouth shape that lies

Strapped to their table. One probes with his ragged nails
  The slate-sharp calf, explores the thigh and the lean
    thews
Of the groin. Others raise, red as piratic sails,
  His wing, stretching, trying the pectoral sinews.

One runs his finger down the wheat of that cruel
  Golden beak, lifts back the horny lids from the eyes,
Peers down in one bright eye, malign as a jewel,
  And steps back suddenly, 'He is anaesthetized?'

'He is. He is. Yes. Yes.' The tallest of them, bent
  Down by the head, rises, 'This drug possesses powers
Sufficient to still all gods in this firmament.
  This is Garuda who was fierce. He's yours for hours.

'We shall continue, please.' Now, once again, he bends
    To the skull, and its clamped tissues. Into the cran-
ial cavity, he plunges both of his hands
    Like obstetric forceps and lifts out the great brain,

Holds it aloft, then gives it to the next who stands
    Beside him. Each, in turn, accepts it, although loath,
Turns it this way, that way, feels it between his hands
    Like a wasps' nest or some sickening outsized growth.

They must decide what thoughts each part of it must think;
    They tap at, then listen beside, each suspect lobe,
Then, with a crow's quill dipped into India ink,
    Mark on its surface, as if on a map or globe,

The dangerous areas which need to be excised.
    They rinse it, then apply antiseptic to it.
And silver saws appear which, inch by inch, slice
    Through its ancient folds and ridges, like thick suet.

It's rinsed, dried, and daubed with thick salves. The smoky
    saws
    Are scrubbed, resterilized, and polished till they gleam.
The brain is repacked in its case. Pinched in their claws,
    Glimmering needles stitch it up, that leave no seam.

Meantime, one of them has set blinders to the eyes,
    Inserted light packing beneath each of the ears
And caulked the nostrils in. One, with thin twine, ties
    The genitals off. With long wooden-handled sheers,

Another chops pinions out of the scarlet wings.
    It's hoped that with disuse he will forget the sky
Or, at least, in time, learn, among other things,
    To fly no higher than his superiors fly.

Well; that's a beginning. The next time, they can split
    His tongue and teach him to talk correctly, can give
Him memory of fine books and choose clothing fit
    For the integrated area where he'll live.

Their candidate may live to give them thanks one day.
 He will recover and may hope for such success
He shall return to join their ranks. Bowing away,
 They nod, whispering, 'One of ours; one of ours. Yes.
  Yes.'

*Phi Beta Kappa poem, 1961, Columbia University*


## Monet: 'Les Nymphéas'

THE eyelids glowing, some chill morning.
O world half-known through opening, twilit lids
 Before the vague face clenches into light;
O universal waters like a cloud,
 Like those first clouds of half-created matter;
O all things rising, rising like the fumes
 From waters falling, O forever falling;
Infinite, the skeletal shells that fall, relinquished,
 The snowsoft sift of the diatoms, like selves
Downdrifting age upon age through milky oceans;
 O slow downdrifting of the atoms;
O island nebulae and O the nebulous islands
 Wandering these mists like falsefires, which are true,
Bobbing like milkweed, like warm lanterns bobbing
 Through the snowfilled windless air, blinking and passing
As we pass into the memory of women
 Who are passing. Within those depths
What ravening? What devouring rage?
 How shall our living know its ends of yielding?
These things have taken me as the mouth an orange –
 That acrid sweet juice entering every cell;
And I am shared out. I become these things:

These lilies, if these things *are* waterlilies
Which are dancers growing dim across no floor;
    These mayflies; whirled dust orbitting in the sun;
This blossoming diffused as rushlights; galactic vapours;
    Fluorescence into which we pass and penetrate;
O soft as the thighs of women;
    O radiance, into which I go on dying. . . .

## Some Trees

THESE are amazing: each
Joining a neighbour, as though speech
Were a still performance.
Arranging by chance

To meet as far this morning
From the world as agreeing
With it, you and I
Are suddenly what the trees try

To tell us we are:
That their merely being there
Means something; that soon
We may touch, love, explain.

And glad not to have invented
Such comeliness, we are surrounded:
A silence already filled with noises,
A canvas on which emerges

A chorus of smiles, a winter morning.
Placed in a puzzling light, and moving,
Our days put on such reticence
These accents seem their own defence.

# The Picture of Little J. A. in a Prospect of Flowers

*'He was spoilt from childhood by the future, which he mastered
rather early and apparently without great difficulty'*
BORIS PASTERNAK

I

DARKNESS falls like a wet sponge
And Dick gives Genevieve a swift punch
In the pyjamas. 'Aroint thee, witch.'
Her tongue from previous ecstasy
Releases thoughts like little hats.

'He clap'd me first during the eclipse.
Afterwards I noted his manner
Much altered. But he sending
At that time certain handsome jewels
I durst not seem to take offence.'

In a far recess of summer
Monks are playing soccer.

II

So far is goodness a mere memory
Or naming of recent scenes of badness
That even these lives, children,
You may pass through to be blessed,
So fair does each invent his virtue.

And coming from a white world, music
Will sparkle at the lips of many who are
Beloved. Then these, as dirty handmaidens
To some transparent witch, will dream
Of a white hero's subtle wooing,
And time shall force a gift on each.

That beggar to whom you gave no cent
Striped the night with his strange descant.

### III

Yet I cannot escape the picture
Of my small self in that bank of flowers:
My head among the blazing phlox
Seemed a pale and gigantic fungus.
I had a hard stare, accepting

Everything, taking nothing,
As though the rolled-up future might stink
As loud as stood the sick moment
The shutter clicked. Though I was wrong,
Still, as the loveliest feelings

Must soon find words, and these, yes,
Displace them, so I am not wrong
In calling this comic version of myself
The true one. For as change is horror,
Virtue is really stubbornness

And only in the light of lost words
Can we imagine our rewards.


## A Vase of Flowers

THE vase is white and would be a cylinder
If a cylinder were wider at the top than at the bottom.
The flowers are red, white and blue.

All contact with the flowers is forbidden.

The white flowers strain upward
Into a pallid air of their references,
Pushed slightly by the red and blue flowers.

If you were going to be jealous of the flowers,
Please forget it.
They mean absolutely nothing to me.

## Thoughts of a Young Girl

'It is such a beautiful day I had to write you a letter
From the tower, and to show I'm not mad:
I only slipped on the cake of soap of the air
And drowned in the bathtub of the world.
You were too good to cry much over me.
And now I let you go. Signed, The Dwarf.'

I passed by late in the afternoon
And the smile still played about her lips
As it has for centuries. She always knows
How to be utterly delightful. Oh my daughter,
My sweetheart, daughter of my late employer, princess,
May you not be long on the way!

## Our Youth

Of bricks . . . Who built it? Like some crazy balloon
When love leans on us
Its nights . . . The velvety pavement sticks to our feet.
The dead puppies turn us back on love.

Where we are. Sometimes
The brick arches led to a room like a bubble, that broke when
   you entered it
And sometimes to a fallen leaf.
We got crazy with emotion, showing how much we knew.

The Arabs took us. We knew
The dead horses. We were discovering coffee,
How it is to be drunk hot, with bare feet
In Canada. And the immortal music of Chopin

Which we had been discovering for several months
Since we were fourteen years old. And coffee grounds,
And the wonder of hands, and the wonder of the day
When the child discovers her first dead hand.

Do you know it? Hasn't she
Observed you too? Haven't you been observed to her?
My, haven't the flowers been? Is the evil
In't? What window? What did you say there?

Heh? Eh? Our youth is dead.
From the minute we discover it with eyes closed
Advancing into mountain light.
Ouch . . . You will never have that young boy,

That boy with the monocle
Could have been your father
He is passing by. No, that other one,
Upstairs. He is the one who wanted to see you.

He is dead. Green and yellow handkerchiefs cover him.
Perhaps he will never rot, I see
That my clothes are dry. I will go.
The naked girl crosses the street.

Blue hampers . . . Explosions,
Ice . . . The ridiculous
Vases of porphyry. All that our youth
Can't use, that it was created for.

It's true we have not avoided our destiny
By weeding out the old people.
Our faces have filled with smoke. We escape
Down the cloud ladder, but the problem has not been solved.

## The Young Prince and the Young Princess

THE grass cuts our feet as we wend our way
Across the meadow – you, a child of thirteen
In a man's business suit far too big for you
A symbol of how long we have been together.

I pick the berries for us to eat
Into a tin can and set it on a stump
Soon or late, lateness comes.
Crows come up out of the west.

I want you to examine this solid block of darkness
In which we are imprisoned. But you say, No,
You are tired. You turn over and sleep.
And I sleep, but in my sleep I hear horses carrying you away.

When the breeze is finished it is morning
Again. Wake up. It is time to start walking
Into the heavenly wilderness. This morning, strangers
Come down to the road to feed us. They are afraid to have
    us come so far.

Night comes, but this time it is a different one.
Your feet scarcely seem to touch the grass
As you walk; you have confidence in me;
Moths bump my incandescent head

And I hear the wind. And so it goes. Some day
We will wake up, having fallen in the night
From a high cliff into the white, precious sky.
You will say, 'That is how we lived, you and I.'

## From *The Avenue Bearing the Initial of Christ into the New World*

### II

THE fishmarket closed, the fishes gone into flesh.
The smelts draped on each other, fat with roe,
The marble cod hacked into chunks on the counter,
Butterfishes mouths still open, still trying to eat,
Porgies with receding jaws hinged apart
In a grimace of dejection, as if like cows
They had died under the sledgehammer, perches
In grass-green armour, spotted squeteagues
In the melting ice meek-faced and croaking no more,
Mud-eating mullets buried in crushed ice,
Tilefishes with scales like chickenfat,
Spanish mackerels, buttercups on the flanks,
Pot-bellied pikes, two-tone flounders
After the long contortion of pushing both eyes
To the brown side that they might look up,
Lying brown side down, like a mass laying-on of hands,
Or the oath-taking of an army.

The only things alive are the carp
That drift in the black tank in the rear,
Kept living for the usual reason, that they have not died,
And perhaps because the last meal was garbage and they
    might begin stinking
On dying, before the customer was halfway home.
They nudge each other, to be netted,
The sweet flesh to be lifted thrashing in the air,
To be slugged, and then to keep on living
While they are opened on the counter.

Fishes do not die exactly, it is more
That they go out of themselves, the visible part
Remains the same, there is little pallor,
Only the cataracted eyes which have not shut ever
Must look through the mist which crazed Homer.

These are the vegetables of the deep,
The Sheol-flowers of darkness, swimmers
Of denser darknesses where the sun's rays bend for the last
    time
And in the sky there burns this shifty jellyfish
That degenerates and flashes and re-forms.

Motes in the eye land is the lid of,
They are plucked out of the green skim milk of the eye.

Fishes are nailed on the wood,
The big Jew stands like Christ, nailing them to the wood,
He scrapes the knife up the grain, the scales fly,
He unnails them, reverses them, nails them again,
Scrapes and the scales fly. He lops off the heads,
Shakes out the guts as if they did not belong in the first
    place,
And they are flesh for the first time in their lives.

Dear Frau —:
    Your husband, —, died in the Camp Hospital on —. May
I express my sincere sympathy on your bereavement. — was
admitted to the Hospital on — with severe symptoms of ex-
haustion, complaining of difficulties in breathing and pains
in the chest. Despite competent medication and devoted
medical attention, it proved impossible, unfortunately, to
keep the patient alive. The deceased voiced no final requests.

                                    Camp Commandant, —

On 5th Street Bunko Certified Embalmer Catholic
Leans in his doorway drawing on a Natural Bloom Cigar.
He looks up the street. Even the Puerto Ricans are Jews
And the Chinese Laundry closes on Saturday.

## Flower-herding Pictures on
## Mount Monadnock

### I

I can support it no longer.
Laughing ruefully at myself
For all I claim to have suffered
I get up. Damned nightmarer!

It is New Hampshire out here,
It is nearly the dawn.
The song of the whipoorwill stops
And the dimension of depth seizes everything.

### II

The song of a peabody-bird goes overhead
Like a needle pushed five times through the air.
It enters the leaves, and comes out little changed.

The air is so still
That as they go off through the trees
The love-songs of birds do not get any fainter.

### III

The last memory I have
Is of a flower which cannot be touched,

Through the bloom of which, all day,
Fly crazed, missing bees.

### IV

As I climb, sweat gets up my nostrils;
For an instant I think I am at the sea.

One summer off Cap Ferrat we watched a black seagull
Straining towards the dawn, we stood in the surf—

Grasshoppers splash up where I step,
The mountain-laurel crashes at my thighs.

### V

There is something joyous in the elegies
Of birds. They seem
Caught up in a formal delight,
Though the mourning dove whistles of despair.

But at last in the thousand elegies
The dead rise in our hearts;
On the brink of our happiness we stop
Like someone on a drunk starting to weep.

### VI

I kneel at a pool, I look through my face
At the bacteria I think I see crawling through the moss.

My face sees me, the water stirs, the face,
Looking preoccupied, gets knocked from its bones.

### VII

I weighed eleven pounds
At birth, having stayed on
Two extra weeks in the womb.
Tempted by room and fresh air,
I came out big as a policeman,
Blue-faced, with narrow red eyes.
It was eight days before the doctor
Would scare my mother with me.

Turning and craning in the vines,
I can make out through the leaves
The old, shimmering nothingness, the sky.

### VIII

Green, scaly moosewoods ascend,
Tenants of the shaken paradise.

At every wind, last night's rain
Comes splattering from the leaves.

It drops in flurries, and lies there,
Like footsteps of some running start.

IX

From a rock, a waterfall,
A single trickle like a strand of wire,
Breaks into beads halfway down.

I know the birds fly off,
But the hug of the earth wraps
With moss their graves and the giant boulders.

X

In the forest I discover a flower.

The invisible life of the thing
Goes up in flames that are invisible,
Like cellophane burning in the sunlight.

It burns up. Its drift is to be nothing.

In its covertness it has a way
Of uttering itself in place of itself,
Its blossoms claim to float in the Empyrean,

A wrathful presence on the blur of the ground.

The appeal to heaven breaks off.
The petals begin to fall, in self-forgiveness.
It is a flower. On this mountainside it is dying.

## Leviathan

THIS is the black sea-brute bulling through wave-wrack,
Ancient as ocean's shifting hills, who in sea-toils
Travelling, who furrowing the salt acres
Heavily, his wake hoary behind him,
Shoulders spouting, the fist of his forehead
Over wastes grey-green crashing, among horses unbroken
From bellowing fields, past bone-wreck of vessels,
Tide-ruin, wash of lost bodies bobbing
No longer sought for, and islands of ice gleaming,
Who ravening the rank flood, wave-marshalling,
Overmastering the dark sea-marches, finds home
And harvest. Frightening to foolhardiest
Mariners, his size were difficult to describe:
The hulk of him is like hills heaving,
Dark, yet as crags of drift-ice, crowns cracking in thunder,
Like land's self by night black-looming, surf churning and
    trailing
Along his shores' rushing, shoal-water boding
About the dark of his jaws; and who should moor at his edge
And fare on afoot would find gates of no gardens,
But the hill of dark underfoot diving,
Closing overhead, the cold deep, and drowning.
He is called Leviathan, and named for rolling,
First created he was of all creatures,
He has held Jonah three days and nights,
He is that curling serpent that in ocean is,
Sea-fright he is, and the shadow under the earth.
Days there are, nonetheless, when he lies
Like an angel, although a lost angel
On the waste's unease, no eye of man moving,

Bird hovering, fish flashing, creature whatever
Who after him came to herit earth's emptiness.
Froth at flanks seething soothes to stillness,
Waits; with one eye he watches
Dark of night sinking last, with one eye dayrise
As at first over foaming pastures. He makes no cry
Though that light is a breath. The sea curling,
Star-climbed, wind-combed, cumbered with itself still
As at first it was, is the hand not yet contented
Of the Creator. And he waits for the world to begin.

## Low Fields and Light

I THINK it is in Virginia, that place
That lies across the eye of my mind now
Like a grey blade set to the moon's roundness,
Like a plain of glass touching all there is.

The flat fields run out to the sea there.
There is no sand, no line. It is autumn.
The bare fields, dark between fences, run
Out to the idle gleam of the flat water.

And the fences go on out, sinking slowly,
With a cow-bird half-way, on a stunted post, watching
How the light slides through them easy as weeds
Or wind, slides over them away out near the sky.

Because even a bird can remember
The fields that were there before the slow
Spread and wash of the edging light crawled
There and covered them, a little more each year.

My father never ploughed there, nor my mother
Waited, and never knowingly I stood there
Hearing the seepage slow as growth, nor knew
When the taste of salt took over the ground.

But you would think the fields were something
To me, so long I stare out, looking
For their shapes or shadows through the matted gleam,
    seeing
Neither what is nor what was, but the flat light rising.


### The Bones

It takes a long time to hear what the sands
Seem to be saying, with the wind nudging them,
And then you cannot put it in words nor tell
Why these things should have a voice. All kinds
Of objects come in over the tide-wastes
In the course of a year, with a throaty
Rattle: weeds, driftwood, the bodies of birds
And of fish, shells. For years I had hardly
Considered shells as being bones, maybe
Because of the sound they could still make, though
I knew a man once who could raise a kind
Of wailing tune out of a flute he had,
Made from a fibula: it was much the same
Register as the shells'; the tune did not
Go on when his breath stopped, though you thought it
    would.
Then that morning, coming on the wreck,
I saw the kinship. No recent disaster
But an old ghost from under a green buoy,
Brought in by the last storm, or one from which
The big wind had peeled back the sand grave
To show what was still left: the bleached, chewed-off
Timbers like the ribs of a man or the jaw-bone
Of some extinct beast. Far down the sands its
Broken cage leaned out, casting no shadow
In the veiled light. There was a man sitting beside it
Eating out of a paper, littering the beach

With the bones of a few more fish, while the hulk
Cupped its empty hand high over him. Only he
And I had come to those sands knowing
That they were there. The rest was bones, whatever
Tunes they made. The bones of things; and of men too
And of man's endeavours whose ribs he had set
Between himself and the shapeless tides. Then
I saw how the sand was shifting like water,
That once could walk. Shells were to shut out the sea,
The bones of birds were built for floating
On air and water, and those of fish were devised
For their feeding depths, while a man's bones were framed
For what? For knowing the sands are here,
And coming to hear them a long time; for giving
Shapes to the sprawled sea, weight to its winds,
And wrecks to plead for its sands. These things are not
Limitless: we know there is somewhere
An end to them, though every way you look
They extend farther than a man can see.


## Small Woman on Swallow Street

FOUR feet up, under the bruise-blue
Fingered hat-felt, the eyes begin. The sly brim
Slips over the sky, street after street, and nobody
Knows, to stop it. It will cover
The whole world, if there is time. Fifty years'
Start in grey the eyes have; you will never
Catch up to where they are, too clever
And always walking, the legs not long but
The boots big with wide smiles of darkness
Going round and round at their tops, climbing.
They are almost to the knees already, where
There should have been ankles to stop them.

So must keep walking all the time, hurry, for
The black sea is down where the toes are
And swallows and swallows all. A big coat
Can help save you. But eyes push you down; never
Meet eyes. There are hands in hands, and love
Follows its furs into shut doors; who
Shall be killed first? Do not look up there:
The wind is blowing the building-tops, and a hand
Is sneaking the whole sky another way, but
It will not escape. Do not look up. God is
On High. He can see you. You will die.

## Grandfather in the Old Men's Home

GENTLE at last, and as clean as ever,
He did not even need drink any more,
And his good sons unbent and brought him
Tobacco to chew, both times when they came
To be satisfied he was well cared for.
And he smiled all the time to remember
Grandmother, his wife, wearing the true faith
Like an iron nightgown, yet brought to birth
Seven times and raising the family
Through her needle's eye while he got away
Down the green river, finding directions
For boats. And himself coming home sometimes
Well-heeled but blind drunk, to hide all the bread
And shoot holes in the bucket while he made
His daughters pump. Still smiled as kindly in
His sleep beside the other clean old men
To see Grandmother, every night the same,
Huge in her age, with her thumbed-down mouth, come
Hating the river, filling with her stare
His gliding dream, while he turned to water,

While the children they both had begotten,
With old faces now, but themselves shrunken
To child-size again, stood ranged at her side,
Beating their little Bibles till he died.


### Views from the High Camp

IN the afternoon, while the wind
Lies down in its halcyon self,
A finger of darkness moving like an oar
Follows me through the blinding fields; in the focus
Of its peculiar radiance I have found
Treasures I did not know I had lost, several
Perhaps still in the future. Among them
This epitaph for someone:

*Discoverer of absences, beloved lamp,*
*You that wait,*
*I have migrated from these footsteps,*
*I, alone, my own sole generation.*

Later, loss will wake like the drowsing birds
And have no word. Here we have watched
The great yellow days turning their spokes
Toward autumn and departure
Through month after month of drought, while daily
The sun has hoisted a long cloud of decision
And hung it in my sight at no distance, in the form
Of a tent full of wind, each cord wrenched in turn.

Be assured that the rain will be released
When it is too late to save the harvest.

## Departure's Girl-friend

Loneliness leapt in the mirrors, but all week
I kept them covered like cages. Then I thought
Of a better thing.

And though it was late night in the city
There I was on my way
To my boat, feeling good to be going, hugging
This big wreath with the words like real
Silver: *Bon Voyage*.

        The night
Was mine but everyone's, like a birthday.
Its fur touched my face in passing. I was going
Down to my boat, my boat,
To see it off, and glad at the thought.
Some leaves of the wreath were holding my hands
And the rest waved good-bye as I walked, as though
They were still alive.

And all went well till I came to the wharf, and no one.

I say no one, but I mean
There was this young man, maybe
Out of the merchant marine,
In some uniform, and I knew who he was; just the same
When he said to me where do you think you're going,
I was happy to tell him.

But he said to me, it isn't your boat,
You don't have one. I said, it's mine, I can prove it:
Look at this wreath, I'm carrying to it,
*Bon Voyage*. He said, This is the stone wharf, lady,
You don't own anything here.

                    And as I
Was turning away, the injustice of it
Lit up the buildings, and there I was
In the other and hated city
Where I was born, where nothing is moored, where
The lights crawl over the stone like flies, spelling now,
Now, and the same fat chances roll
Their many eyes; and I step once more
Through a hoop of tears and walk on, holding this
Buoy of flowers in front of my beauty,
Wishing myself the good voyage.

## A Gesture by a Lady with an Assumed Name

LETTERS she left to clutter up the desk
Burned in the general gutter when the maid
Came in to do the room and take the risk
Of slipping off the necklace round her head.

Laundry she left to clutter up the floor
Hung to rachitic skeletons of girls
Who worked the bars or laboured up the stair
To crown her blowsy ribbons on their curls.

Lovers she left to clutter up the town
Mourned in the chilly morgue and went away,
All but the husbands sneaking up and down
The stairs of that apartment house all day.

What were they looking for? The cold pretence
Of lamentation offered in a stew?
A note? A gift? A shred of evidence
To love when there was nothing else to do?

Or did they rise to weep for that unheard-
Of love, whose misery cries and does not care
Whether or not the madam hears a word
Or skinny children watch the trodden stair?

Whether or not, how could she love so many,
Then turn away to die as though for none?
I saw the last offer a child a penny
To creep outside and see the cops were gone.

## At Thomas Hardy's Birthplace, 1953

### I

THE nurse carried him up the stair
Into his mother's sleeping room.
The beeches lashed the roof and dragged the air
    Because of storm.

Wind could have overturned the dead.
Moth and beetle and housefly crept
Under the door to find the lamp, and cowered:
    But still he slept.

The ache and sorrow of darkened earth
Left pathways soft and meadows sodden;
The small Frome overflowed the firth,
    And he lay hidden

In the arms of the tall woman gone
To soothe his mother during the dark;
Nestled against the awkward flesh and bone
    When the rain broke.

### II

Last night at Stinsford where his heart
Is buried now, the rain came down.
Cold to the hidden joy, the secret hurt,
    His heart is stone.

But over the dead leaves in the wet
The mouse goes snooping, and the bird.
Something the voiceless earth does not forget
    They come to guard,

Maybe, the heart who would not tell
Whatever secret he learned from the ground,
Who turned aside and heard the human wail,
    That other sound.

More likely, though, the labouring feet
Of fieldmouse, hedgehog, moth and hawk
Seek in the storm what comfort they can get
   Under the rock

Where surely the heart will not wake again
To endure the unending beat of the air,
Having been nursed beyond the sopping rain,
   Back down the stair.


### Saint Judas

WHEN I went out to kill myself, I caught
A pack of hoodlums beating up a man.
Running to spare his suffering, I forgot
My name, my number, how my day began,
How soldiers milled around the garden stone
And sang amusing songs; how all that day
Their javelins measured crowds; how I alone
Bargained the proper coins, and slipped away.

Banished from heaven, I found this victim beaten,
Stripped, kneed, and left to cry. Dropping my rope
Aside, I ran, ignored the uniforms:
Then I remembered bread my flesh had eaten,
The kiss that ate my flesh. Flayed without hope,
I held the man for nothing in my arms.

JAMES WRIGHT

## Confession to J. Edgar Hoover

HIDING in the church of an abandoned stone,
A Negro soldier
Is flipping the pages of the Articles of War,
That he can't read.

Our father,
Last evening I devoured the wing
Of a cloud.
And, in the city, I sneaked down
To pray with a sick tree.

I labour to die, father,
I ride the great stones,
I hide under stars and maples,
And yet I cannot find my own face.
In the mountains of blast furnaces,
The trees turn their backs on me.

Father, the dark moths
Crouch at the sills of earth, waiting.

And I am afraid of my own prayers.
Father, forgive me.
I did not know what I was doing.

## Lying in a Hammock at William Duffy's Farm in Pine Island, Minnesota

OVER my head, I see the bronze butterfly,
Asleep on the black trunk,
Blowing like a leaf in green shadow.
Down the ravine behind the empty house,
The cowbells follow one another
Into the distances of the afternoon.
To my right,
In a field of sunlight between two pines,
The droppings of last year's horses
Blaze into golden stones.
I lean back, as the evening darkens and comes on.
A chicken-hawk floats over, looking for home.
I have wasted my life.

## Depressed by a Book of Bad Poetry, I walk toward an Unused Pasture and Invite the Insects to Join Me

RELIEVED, I let the book fall behind a stone.
I climb a slight rise of grass.
I do not want to disturb the ants
Who are walking single file up the fence post,
Carrying small white petals,
Casting shadows so frail that I can see through them.
I close my eyes for a moment, and listen.
The old grasshoppers
Are tired, they leap heavily now,
Their thighs are burdened.
I want to hear them, they have clear sounds to make.
They have gone to sleep.
Then lovely, far off, a dark cricket begins
In the castles of maple.

## The Blessing

JUST off the highway to Rochester, Minnesota,
Twilight bounds softly forth on the grass.
And the eyes of those two Indian ponies
Darken with kindness.
They have come gladly out of the willows
To welcome my friend and me.
We step over the barbed wire into the pasture
Where they have been grazing all day, alone.
They ripple tensely, they can hardly contain their happiness
That we have come.
They bow shyly as wet swans. They love each other.
There is no loneliness like theirs.
At home once more,
They begin munching the young tufts of spring in the
    darkness.
I would like to hold the slenderer one in my arms,
For she has walked over to me
And nuzzled my left hand.
She is black and white,
Her mane falls wild on her forehead,
And the light breeze moves me to caress her long ear
That is delicate as the skin over a girl's wrist.
Suddenly I realize
That if I stepped out of my body I would break
Into blossom.

## *Miners*

THE police are dragging for the bodies
Of miners in the black waters
Of the suburbs.

Below, some few
Crawl, searching, until they clasp
The fingers of the sea.

Somewhere,
Beyond ripples and drowsing woodchucks,
A strong man, alone,
Beats on the door of a grave, crying
*Oh let me in.*

Many women mount long stairs
Into the shafts,
And emerge in the tottering palaces
Of abandoned cisterns.

In the middle of the night,
I can hear cars, moving on steel rails, colliding
Underground.

## First Confession

BLOOD thudded in my ears. I scuffed,
  Steps stubborn, to the telltale booth
Beyond whose curtained portal coughed
  The robed repositor of truth.

The slat shot back. The universe
  Bowed down his cratered dome to hear
Enumerated my each curse,
  The sip snitched from my old man's beer,

My sloth pride envy lechery,
  The dime held back from Peter's Pence
With which I'd bribed my girl to pee
  That I might spy her instruments.

Hovering scale-pans when I'd done
  Settled their balance slow as silt
While in the restless dark I burned
  Bright as a brimstone in my guilt

Until as one feeds birds he doled
  Seven Our Fathers and a Hail
Which I to double-scrub my soul
  Intoned twice at the altar rail

Where Sunday in seraphic light
  I knelt, as full of grace as most,
And stuck my tongue out at the priest:
  A fresh roost for the Holy Ghost.

## Nude Descending a Staircase

Toe upon toe, a snowing flesh,
A gold of lemon, root and rind,
She sifts in sunlight down the stairs
With nothing on. Nor on her mind.

We spy beneath the banister
A constant thresh of thigh on thigh—
Her lips imprint the swinging air
That parts to let her parts go by.

One-woman waterfall, she wears
Her slow descent like a long cape
And pausing, on the final stair
Collects her motions into shape.

## Little Elegy
#### for a child who skipped rope

Here lies resting, out of breath,
Out of turns, Elizabeth
Whose quicksilver toes not quite
Cleared the whirring edge of night.

Earth whose circles round us skim
Till they catch the lightest limb,
Shelter now Elizabeth
And for her sake trip up death.

## B Negative

M | 60 | 5 FT 4 | W PROT

You know it's April by the falling-off
In coughdrop boxes – fewer people cough –
   By daisies' first white eyeballs in the grass
And every dawn more underthings cast off.

Though plumtrees stretch recovered boughs to us
And doubledecked in green, the downtown bus,
   Love in one season – so your stab-pole tells –
Beds down, and buds, and is deciduous.

Now set down burlap bag. In pigeon talk
The wobbling pigeon flutes on the sidewalk,
   Struts on the breeze and clicks leisurely wings
As if the corn he ate grew on a stalk.

So plump he topples where he tries to stand,
He pecks my shoelaces, come to demand
   Another sack, another fifteen cents,
And yet – who else will eat out of my hand?

It used to be that when I laid my head
And body with it down by you in bed
   You did not turn from me nor fall to sleep
But turn to fall between my arms instead

And now I lay bifocals down. My feet
Forget the twist that brought me to your street.
   I can't make out your face for steamed-up glass
Nor quite call back your outline on the sheet.

I know how, bent to a movie magazine,
The hobo's head lights up, and from its screen
   Imagined bosoms in slow motion bloom
And no director interrupts the scene.

I used to purchase in the Automat
A cup of soup and fan it with my hat
    Until a stern voice from the changebooth crashed
Like nickels: *Gentlemen do not do that.*

Spring has no household, no abiding heat,
Pokes forth no bud from branches of concrete,
    Nothing to touch you, nothing you can touch —
The snow, at least, keeps track of people's feet.

The springer spaniel and the buoyant hare
Seem half at home reclining in mid-air —
    But, Lord, the times I've leaped the way they do
And looked round for a foothold — in despair.

The subway a little cheaper than a room,
I browse the *News* — or so the guards assume —
    And there half-waking, tucked in funny-sheets,
I hurtle in my mileaminute womb.

Down streets that wake up earlier than wheels
The routed spirit flees on dusty heels
    And in the soft fire of a muscatel
Sits up, puts forth its fingertips, and feels —

Down streets so deep the sun can't vault their walls,
Where one-night wives make periodic calls,
    Where cat steals stone where rat makes off with child
And lyre and lute lie down under three balls,

Down blocks in sequence, fact by separate fact,
The human integers add and subtract
    Till in a cubic room in some hotel
You wake one day to find yourself abstract

And turn a knob and hear a voice: *Insist
On Jiffy Blades, they're tender to the wrist —*
    Then static, then a squawk as if your hand
Had shut a human windpipe with a twist.

I know how, lurking under trees by dark,
Poor loony stranglers out to make their mark
    Reach forth shy hands to touch some woman's hair –
I pick up after them in Central Park.

## In a Prominent Bar in Secaucus One Day

(*To the tune of 'The Old Orange Flute' or the tune of 'Sweet
Betsy from Pike'*)

In a prominent bar in Secaucus one day
Rose a lady in skunk with a topheavy sway,
Raised a knobby red finger – all turned from their beer –
While with eyes bright as snowcrust she sang high and clear:

'Now who of you'd think from an eyeload of me
That I once was a lady as proud as could be?
Oh I'd never sit down by a tumbledown drunk
If it wasn't, my dears, for the high cost of junk.

'All the gents used to swear that the white of my calf
Beat the down of the swan by a length and a half.
In the kerchief of linen I caught to my nose
Ah, there never fell snot, but a little gold rose.

'I had seven gold teeth and a toothpick of gold,
My Virginia cheroot was a leaf of it rolled
And I'd light it each time with a thousand in cash –
Why the bums used to fight if I flicked them an ash.

'Once the toast of the Biltmore, the belle of the Taft,
I would drink bottle beer at the Drake. never draught,
And dine at the Astor on Salisbury steak
With a clean tablecloth for each bite I did take.

'In a car like the Roxy I'd roll to the track,
A steel-guitar trio, a bar in the back,
And the wheels made no noise, they turned over so fast,
Still it took you ten minutes to see me go past.

'When the horses bowed down to me that I might choose,
I bet on them all, for I hated to lose.
Now I'm saddled each night for my butter and eggs
And the broken threads race down the backs of my legs.

'Let you hold in mind, girls, that your beauty must pass
Like a lovely white clover that rusts with its grass.
Keep your bottoms off barstools and marry you young
Or be left – an old barrel with many a bung.

'For when time takes you out for a spin in his car
You'll be hard-pressed to stop him from going too far
And be left by the roadside, for all your good deeds,
Two toadstools for tits and a face full of weeds.'

All the house raised a cheer, but the man at the bar
Made a phonecall and up pulled a red patrol car
And she blew us a kiss as they copped her away
From that prominent bar in Secaucus, N. J.

## The Insusceptibles

THEN the long sunlight lying on the sea
Fell, folded gold on gold; and slowly we
Took up our decks of cards, our parasols,
The picnic hamper and the sandblown shawls
And climbed the dunes in silence. There were two
Who lagged behind as lovers sometimes do,
And took a different road. For us the night
Was final, and by artificial light
We came indoors to sleep. No envy there
Of those who might be watching anywhere
The lustres of the summer dark, to trace
Some vagrant splinter blazing out of space.
No thought of them, save in a lower room
To leave a light for them when they should come.

## Readings of History

*'He delighted in relating the fact that he had been born near Girgenti
in a place called Chaos during a raging cholera epidemic'*

DOMENICO VITTORINI,
*The Drama of Luigi Pirandello*

I

### The Evil Eye

LAST night we sat with the stereopticon,
laughing at genre view of 1906,
till suddenly, gazing straight into
that fringed and tasselled parlour, where the vestal
spurns an unlikely suitor

with hairy-crested plants to right and left,
my heart sank. It was terrible.
I smelled the mildew in those swags of plush,
dust on the eyepiece bloomed to freaks of mould.
I knew beyond all doubt how dead that couple was.

Today, a fresh clean morning.
Your camera stabs me unawares,
right in my mortal part.
A womb of celluloid already
contains my dotage and my total absence.

## II

### *The Confrontation*

Luigi Pirandello
looked like an old historian
(oval head, tufted white beard,
not least the hunger
for reconciliation in his eye).
For fourteen years, facing
his criminal reflection
in his wife's Grand Guignol mind,
he built over and over
that hall of mirrors
in which to be appears
to be perceived.

The present holds you like a raving wife,
clever as the mad are clever,
digging up your secret truths
from her disabled genius.
She knows what you hope
and dare not hope:
remembers
what you're sick of forgetting.

What are you now
but what you know together, you and she?
She will not let you think.
It is important to get away
to make connexions. Everything
happens very fast in the minds
of the insane. Even you
aren't up to that, yet.
Go out, walk,
think of selves long past.

### III

*Memorabilia*

I recall
Civil War letters of a great-grand-uncle,
fifteen at Chancellorsville,

                    no raconteur,
no speller, either; nor, to put it squarely,
much of a mind;

               the most we gather
is that he did write home:

                  *I am well,*
*how are my sisters, hope you are the same.*
Did Spartan battle-echoes rack his head?
Dying, he turned into his father's memory.

History's queerly strong perfumes
rise from the crook of this day's elbow:
Seduction fantasies of the public mind,
or Dilthey's dream from which he roused to see
the cosmos glaring through his windowpane?
Prisoners of what we think occurred,
or dreamers dreaming toward a final word?

What, in fact, happened in these woods
on some obliterated afternoon?

IV

*Consanguinity*

Can history show us nothing
but pieces of ourselves, detached,
set to a kind of poetry,
a kind of music, even?
Seated today on Grandmamma's
plush sofa with the grapes
bursting so ripely from the curved mahogany,
we read the great Victorians
weeping, almost, as if
some family breach were healed.
Those angry giantesses and giants,
lately our kith and kin!
We stare into their faces, hear
at last what they were saying
(or some version not bruited
by filial irritation).

The cat-tails wither in the reading-room.
Tobacco-coloured dust
drifts on the newest magazines.
I skulk here leafing ancient copies
of LIFE from World War II.
We look so poor and honest there:
girls with long hair badly combed
and unbecoming dresses –
where are you now?
                            You sail
to shop in Europe, ignorantly saved
for you, an age ago.
Your nylon luggage matches
                                        eyelids
expertly azured.
I, too, have lived in history.

V

*The Mirror*

Is it in hopes
to find or lose myself
that I
fill up my table now
with Michelet and Motley?
to 'know how it was'
or to forget how it is –
what else?
Split at the root, neither Gentile nor Jew,
Yankee nor Rebel, born
in the face of two ancient cults,
I'm a good reader of histories.
And you,
Morris Cohen, dear to me as a brother,
when you sit at night
tracing your way through your volumes
of Josephus, or any
of the old Judaic chronicles,
do you find yourself there, a simpler
more eloquent Jew?
                          or do you read
to shut out the tick-tock of self,
the questions and their routine answers?

VI

*The Covenant*

The present breaks our hearts. We lie and freeze,
our fingers icy as a bunch of keys.
Nothing will thaw these bones except
memory like an ancient blanket wrapped
about us when we sleep at home again,
smelling of picnics, closets, sicknesses,

old nightmare,
                    and insomnia's spreading stain.
Or say I sit with what I halfway know
as with a dying man who heaves the true
version at last, now that it hardly matters,
or gropes a hand to where the letters
sewn in the mattress can be plucked and read.
Here's water.   Sleep.   No more is asked of you.
I take your life into my living head.

*Phi Beta Kappa poem, 1960, College of William and Mary*

## All through the Rains

THAT mare stood in the field –
A big pine-tree and a shed,
But she stayed in the open
Ass to the wind, splash wet.
I tried to catch her April
For a bareback ride,
She kicked and bolted
Later grazing fresh shoots
In the shade of the down
Eucalyptus on the hill.


## Piute Creek

ONE granite ridge
A tree, would be enough
Or even a rock, a small creek,
A bark-shred in a pool.
Hill beyond hill, folded and twisted
Tough trees crammed
In thin stone fractures
A huge moon on it all, is too much.
The mind wanders. A million
Summers, night air still and the rocks
Warm. Sky over endless mountains.
All the junk that goes with being human
Drops away, hard rock wavers
Even the heavy present seems to fail
This bubble of a heart.

Words and books
Like a small creek off a high ledge
Gone in the dry air.
A clear, attentive mind
Has no meaning but that
Which sees is truly seen.
No one loves rock, yet we are here.
Night chills. A flick
In the moonlight
Slips into Juniper shadow:
Back there unseen
Cold proud eyes
Of Cougar or Coyote
Watch me rise and go.


## Above Pate Valley

WE finished clearing the last
Section of trail by noon,
High on the ridge-side
Two thousand feet above the creek –
Reached the pass, went on
Beyond the white pine groves,
Granite shoulders, to a small
Green meadow watered by the snow,
Edged with Aspen – sun
Straight high and blazing
But the air was cool.
Ate a cold fried trout in the
Trembling shadows. I spied
A glitter, and found a flake
Black volcanic glass – obsidian –
By a flower. Hands and knees

Pushing the Bear grass, thousands
Of arrowhead leavings over a
Hundred yards. Not one good
Head, just razor flakes
On a hill snowed all but summer,
A land of fat summer deer,
They came to camp. On their
Own trails. I followed my own
Trail here. Picked up the cold-drill,
Pick, singlejack, and sack
Of dynamite.
Ten thousand years.


## Milton by Firelight
### (Piute Creek, August 1955)

'O HELL, what do mine eyes
   with grief behold?'
Working with an old
Singlejack miner, who can sense
The vein and cleavage
In the very guts of rock, can
Blast granite, build
Switchbacks that last for years
Under the beat of snow, thaw, mule-hooves.
What use, Milton, a silly story
Of our lost general parents,
   eaters of fruit?

The Indian, the chainsaw boy,
And a string of six mules
Came riding down to camp
Hungry for tomatoes and green apples.

Sleeping in saddle-blankets
Under a bright night-sky
Han River slantwise by morning.
Jays squall
Coffee boils

In ten thousand years the Sierras
Will be dry and dead, home of the scorpion.
Ice-scratched slabs and bent trees.
No paradise, no fall,
Only the weathering land
The wheeling sky,
Man, with his Satan
Scouring the chaos of the mind.
Oh Hell!

Fire down
Too dark to read, miles from a road
The bell-mare clangs in the meadow
That packed dirt for a fill-in
Scrambling through loose rocks
On an old trail
All of a summer's day.

## Hay for the Horses

HE had driven half the night
From far down San Joaquin
Through Mariposa, up the
Dangerous mountain roads,
And pulled in at eight a.m.
With his big truckload of hay
            behind the barn.

With winch and ropes and hooks
We stacked the bales up clean
To splintery redwood rafters
High in the dark, flecks of alfalfa
Whirling through shingle-cracks of light,
Itch of haydust in the
                sweaty shirt and shoes.
At lunchtime under Black oak
Out in the hot corral,
– The old mare nosing lunchpails,
Grasshoppers crackling in the weeds –
'I'm sixty-eight,' he said,
'I first bucked hay when I was seventeen.
I thought, that day I started,
I sure would hate to do this all my life.
And dammit, that's just what
I've gone and done.'

# ROBERT MEZEY

## The Funeral Home

In the environs of the funeral home
The smell of death was absent. All I knew
Were flowers rioting and odours blown
Tangible as a blossom into the face,
To be inhaled and hushed – and where they grew
Smothered the nostrils in the pungent grass.

Hyacinths of innocence, and yellow-hammers,
That beat the air at dawn, at dusk, to metal
Immortality, that flush where a bee clamours
For wine, are blooms of another colour. See
How the flush fades as it descends the petal,
How deep the insect drinks, how quietly.

And curious, that among these ferns and rocks,
The violets flying a modest and blue elation,
And flapping ruffles of the white lilacs,
Shaking the air to tempt the golden bee,
Stiffen at the moment of consummation,
Swayed with guilt and weight of the bee's body.

These flowers, when cut and used, will remain ruddy,
As though made deathless in the very way
Their cutter kept the hue in the human body
That they were cut to celebrate and mourn.
The coffin has sprouted in dark mahogany
Out of them – edged, and shining like a thorn.

## Epitaph of a Faithful Man

You of the covered breasts, the lovely head,
Must now be withered, or like me, a ghost —
Say that some women had of me a token
Of that long love which you alone could boast;
Say that I slept in many another's bed —
I sleep here now, my oath still unbroken.

## Late Winter Birthday

This broken city, heaving a white breath
As if in preparation for a truce,
Gathers the sleeping folk, their flesh gone loose,
About its frozen shoulders. In sleep or death,
Their bodies are the start I waken with.
I see my image totter and the bruise
Of every hour infect the wind and freeze;
My history leaves its crystals in my mouth.

The lamps go out as if they fear the dawn.
I sit reading, watching beyond the sill
Morning in naked indigo waken the snows
To aimless forage. Somewhere, with measured blows,
A large, black bell is beating what is gone
Into the splintered forest of my will.

## Dark Head

DARK head, your heavy sleep, the gift
Of passion loosed in the light an hour,
Remembers well what shadowy thing
Turned earthward in a golden shower.

Your mingled fragrances in sleep –
The breath of ferns, the salt of ocean –
The closeness of our arms and legs,
And the clear sweat of their commotion

Move me to wish that time would cease,
Your face in this wild and surging light
Grow final, and our pact remain
Unalterable. No chance of that.

Let me be different where you lie
Beyond possession still, beyond
The small cage of my heart, its sick
Persistence for eternal blonde,

And turn my barren hungers down,
Love's shabby kinsmen. It is night,
And summer, and the wind is dense
With rain and questions. By what right

Will any be as we have been?
And will we be when we are old?
Sleep, Mary, sleep. An older wind
Is rising, and the rain is cold.

ROBERT MEZEY

## The Lovemaker

I SEE you in her bed,
Dark, rootless epicene,
Where a lone ghost is laid
And other ghosts convene;

And hear you moan at last
Your pleasure in the deep
Haven of her who kissed
Your blind mouth into sleep.

But the body, once enthralled,
Wakes in the chains it wore,
Dishevelled, stupid, cold,
And famished as before—

And hears its paragon
Breathe in the ghostly air,
Anonymous carrion,
Ravished by despair.

Lovemaker, I have felt
Desire taking my part,
But lacked your constant fault
And something of your art,

Unwilling to bend my knees
To such unmantled pride
As left you in that place,
Restless, dissatisfied.

ROBERT MEZEY

## To Philip Levine, on the Day of Atonement

IMPENITENT, we meet again,
As Gentile as your wife or mine,
And pour into affection's cup
Secular California wine.

Jewless in Gaza, we have come
Where worldly likenesses commence
And gather fury, but still keep
Some dark, essential difference.

Is it the large, unchiselled nose,
That monument to daily breath?
Is it some fibre in the heart,
That makes the heart believe in death?

God only knows. And who is he?
The cold comedian of our harm?
I wear its badge upon my sleeve,
You, like a scar on either arm —

But neither knows what good it does.
A voiceless darkness falls again
On this elaborate wilderness
And fills the empty minds of men

Where they sit drinking with their wives,
Children asleep, but not in bed,
Nothing to atone for but the cold
And blurred perspectives of the dead.

# INDEX OF TITLES

# INDEX OF POETS

# INDEX OF FIRST LINES

INDEX OF FIRST LINES

198

# INDEX OF FIRST LINES

*Some other volumes in the
Penguin Poets are described
on the following
pages*

# THE PENGUIN BOOK OF
# RUSSIAN VERSE

### Edited by Dimitri Obolensky

The belief, current in the West, that Russian poetry has its beginnings in the early nineteenth century is, though misguided, understandable. The unexampled blossoming of this poetry between 1810 and 1830, in a newly developed language easily recognizable as modern Russian and in a literary context avowedly European, makes the age of Pushkin seem like a sudden flowering in a wilderness Eighteenth-century Russian literature, without which Pushkin himself cannot be properly understood, is in the West largely unknown or dismissed as derivative and 'pseudo-classical'; while further back, the Russian Middle Ages extend in an ill-defined penumbra, out of which inexplicably emerge a number of heroic poems transmitted by word of mouth from generation to generation, some of which have been translated into languages of Western Europe.

This collection of Russian verse, which extends from heroic poems of the twelfth century to the work of poets still living, is accompanied by plain prose translations and an excellent introduction.

# BAUDELAIRE

## Edited by Francis Scarfe

A poet whose work is so complex and diverse, though apparently so simple and unified, as Baudelaire's is not to be summarized in any convenient formula. Yet many attempts of this kind have been made; they are useful and have to be taken seriously. A modern Dante? This suggestion, first made in 1857 by Thierry, has been discussed and modified by T. S. Eliot who would be more satisfied with a comparison with Goethe. 'The Swift of poetry', Lytton Strachey neatly suggested: but they meet only in their disgust, wit, and gloom, and Baudelaire is the bigger of the two. Aldous Huxley called him 'a bored satanist' and Lionel Johnson stated: 'Baudelaire sings sermons.' He has been described as 'the tragic sophist', as 'Too Christian', and as a 'Near-Jansenist'.

In this selection Francis Scarfe has placed the poems, for the first time, in a roughly chronological order while trying to preserve the 'cycles' into which they fall. A plain prose translation is appended to each poem.

# SWINBURNE

### Selected and introduced by Bonamy Dobrée

It is now over fifty years since Swinburne died, and nearly a hundred years since his poetry flamed into the heads and bosoms of the poetry-reading public of the day. Young men in the 1860s would go about 'chanting to one another the new astonishing melodies' of the choruses in *Atalanta in Calydon*, or verses from the first *Poems and Ballads*.

No selection of Swinburne can be satisfactory to everybody, least of all, possibly, to him who selects. What Bonamy Dobrée has tried to do in this edition is to exemplify as far as may be every aspect of his poetry (avoiding for the most part the very long poems, though with regret); the passionate, the contemplative, the complex, and the simple, contrasting those packed with ideas and the more easily assimilated narrative pieces, the vivid and the incantatory. The result is an excellent selection from the works of a poet whose surging rhythms and alliterative effects made so great an impression on the late Victorians.

# PENGUIN POETS

There are over thirty volumes in Penguin Poets, which include selections from the work of individual poets, anthologies of English, British Commonwealth, and foreign poetry, and three books of comic and curious verse. Recent additions include:

**THE PENGUIN BOOK OF JAPANESE VERSE**
*Edited by Geoffrey Bownas*

**GOETHE**
*Edited by David Luke*

**THE PENGUIN BOOK OF SICK VERSE**
*Edited by George MacBeth*

**PUSHKIN**
*Edited by John Fennell*

*Also available:*

**THE PENGUIN BOOK OF SPANISH VERSE**

**THE PENGUIN BOOK OF FRENCH VERSE**
(in 4 volumes)

**THE PENGUIN BOOK OF GERMAN VERSE**

**THE PENGUIN BOOK OF ITALIAN VERSE**

**THE PENGUIN BOOK OF CHINESE VERSE**

In Penguin Poets all volumes of foreign poetry contain English prose translations